god bless you
Trevor
Hendershot

ANGEL FOR HIGHER

Robert Hendershot

with

Trevor Hendershot

Revised, Reformatted and Redeemed Edition
Originally Published as *Trevorized!* in 2015

Copyright © 2017 Robert Hendershot

Cover Photos & Graphic Design Credit:
Kirk Phillips, Taylor Hendershot, and Tim Brillhart

ISBN: 1543058299

ISBN-13: 978-1543058291

TO MY BEAUTIFUL WIFE, MELISSA: You've always been the foundation of our family, keeping us together throughout the many trials and triumphs we've experienced during our thirty years of marriage. Your sacrificial love, irreplaceable friendship, and insightful discernment have taught me by example that I needed to put Jesus first if I wanted our marriage to last; that while our marriage may have been made in heaven, we still have to work on it while we remain on earth; and finally, that the only things wrong with our marriage today are those things that God could have fixed in *me* yesterday.

> Grow old along with me!
> The best is yet to be,
> The last of life, for which the first was made:
> Our times are in His hand
> Who saith, "A whole I planned,
> Youth shows but half; trust God: see all, nor be afraid!"

> —Robert Browning, 1812–1889

* * *

TO OUR THREE AMAZING SONS, TREVOR, TAYLOR, AND TANNER: You are all an incredible heritage from the Lord and a priceless, though undeserved, reward from Him. We will continue to pray daily that your thoughts, words, and actions would always glorify God and that your needs, wants, and desires would always be in harmony with His good, pleasing, and perfect will for your lives.

> Sons are a heritage from the Lord,
>   children a reward from Him.
> Like arrows in the hands of a warrior
>   are sons born in one's youth.
> Blessed is the man
>   whose quiver is full of them.
> They will not be put to shame
>   when they contend with their enemies in the gate.

> (Psalm 127:3–5)

CONTENTS

FOREWORD

I've just finished reading my friend Robert Hendershot's recently revised book, *Angel for Higher.* My first response even before reading his manuscript was that I was humbled that Robert would invite me to write the foreword to his book. Robert and Trevor are a vital part of our men's ministry and a tremendous blessing to all who attend our Friday morning Influencers meetings of over two hundred men in Irvine, California.

After reading Robert's manuscript, I can say that I'm blessed and honored to be able to encourage others to read Robert and Trevor's inspiring story. I was very pleasantly surprised to discover that Robert is a gifted writer and storyteller. I found myself laughing until I cried and crying until I laughed. I literally couldn't stop reading it!

Not only is it both amusing and interesting but it's also filled with spiritual principles and lessons from their lives that I know will encourage those currently suffering with any tribulation in their own lives. The message of how our good God can take the pain we feel and the messes we make and turn them into our greatest blessings comes through loud and clear throughout this book. It overflows with both the absolute hope and amazing grace that this hurting and confused world so desperately needs.

This is a book for everyone, but it might be especially inspirational for anyone who has a child with a disability, or a relative or friend who might have such a child. I believe it will also be edifying for many to hear how God uniquely dealt with Robert during his recovery from alcoholism. Sober now for over twenty years, the biblical truths that Robert learned and passes along not only gave him a wonderfully new quality of life but they also taught him valuable lessons that helped him become a better parent to Trevor.

Robert also helped me to understand, in many insightful ways, how concerned people can assist the hurting friends or family members in their own lives to better cope with whatever spiritual, emotional, or physical problems they are facing. As I've already said, I believe this is a book for everyone, and so even if having a disabled person or someone recovering from an addiction in your life is not your current situation, Robert and Trevor's story of how God was able to turn their tears of great sadness into tears of great joy will be a source of tremendous blessing to all who read it.

But the absolute best reason for reading this book is to be inspired by the way Robert communicates and instructs through his life experiences about what a great God he has and what a wonderful Savior he has in Jesus Christ. He does this with heart and depth on every page through many humorous, transparent, and practical ways. He also gives a clear presentation of how we can know God and access His power and joy in overcoming the difficult situations we all face in our lives at one time or another. God, and God alone, is the only credible explanation for the miracles of love, grace, and mercy displayed in the lives of Robert and Trevor.

In a world flying apart at the seams, in a country in crisis on every front, and in hurting families across this nation, the personal solutions that Robert and Trevor have found in their relationship with Jesus Christ are available to anyone who is searching for truthful answers to the challenges in their lives. For that reason alone, I highly recommend *Angel for Higher.* I guarantee you'll enjoy it!

Pete McKenzie
Western Director, Influencers Men's Ministry

PREFACE

Angel for Higher chronicles two lives characterized by faith in God, recovery from alcoholism, and living with a disability. The life of my son Trevor, who has Down syndrome, and my life as a sober alcoholic both testify how God can take what we learn through overcoming earlier suffering in our lives and synergistically use those lessons to enable us to triumph over subsequent, and sometimes even greater, challenges later in our lives.

> If you have raced with men on foot
>> and they have worn you out,
>> how can you compete with horses?
> If you stumble in safe country,
>> how will you manage in the thickets by the Jordan?

(Jeremiah 12:5)

The spiritual understanding of God's purposes *for*, as well as the practical solutions *to*, the obstacles in our lives that Trevor and I gained through our "Synergy of Suffering" experiences are accessible to anyone who is contending with a disability, addiction, or any other seemingly insurmountable challenge. *Angel for Higher* will hopefully encourage you to cry out to God in your times of trouble with an SOS prayer of your own for the wisdom and discernment to help you to understand the divine reason for your suffering, as well as to provide you with the strength and resources you need to overcome whatever difficulties you are facing in your life.

> But those who suffer He delivers in their suffering;
> He speaks to them in their affliction.

> (Job 36:15)

My greatest prayer is that *Angel for Higher* will influence you to appreciate the unequivocal fact that God has absolutely created each and every human being to be incredibly precious, infinitely valuable, and eternally significant in His sight.

Robert Hendershot
January 15, 2017

PROLOGUE:

FATHER'S DAY TESTIMONY

Voyagers Bible Church

June 17, 1990

Good morning. I'm Bob Hendershot. While I imagine not many of you here may know me by sight, I believe many more of you have at least heard about Trevor, Melissa, and myself, because I know for a fact that a whole lot of you have been praying for us. This is not going to be easy for me, but I wanted to take a minute or two to thank all of you for all the prayers we've received over the last forty-five days or so.

Last Sunday was the first time all three of us were able to make it to church at the same time—Melissa and Trevor are coming to the second service today—but I have to tell you that thanks to your prayers, every day has felt like Sunday at our house.

For those of you who don't know, Trevor was born on May 4, and as of today, physically, he's doing fantastic. He eats well . . . has a good heart—we're very fortunate. Developmentally, however, the Lord has given us—and ultimately Trevor—an additional challenge. Now when you've tried for so very long to become parents—daily prayer, monthly heartbreak, and five years of disappointment—and then you at last see your first and most likely only child being born, and the doctor tells you, "He's a boy," that was the happiest moment of my life.

But when that same doctor, five minutes later, asked me, "Do you know what Down syndrome is?" that was by far the saddest moment of my life. Let me tell you, to go from utter joy to utter devastation in the five seconds it took for the doctor to finish her question was the hardest thing I've ever had to endure. While I already had a general idea of what it meant to have Down syndrome, I've learned a whole lot more over the last few weeks by reading books, talking to other parents, and just observing Trevor. Without getting too technical, it does mean that Trevor will be delayed in his development, although we're not sure exactly how much or how high a plateau he will eventually reach. God knows, and time will tell.

Now when I think of all the men and women in this church today—those of you who have great hope, solid belief, and tremendous faith—well, some of you have been Christians for many years, and a few practically all of your lives. If you would've asked me seven weeks ago which couple was best qualified to handle a challenge like this, I know that Melissa and I would be down at the bottom of the list. The fact of the matter is we could not have handled it without the prayers I've already mentioned but also the support—the practical, physical, hands-on support—we've received from all of you in the way of cards, phone calls, and just actually being available to help us bear this burden in any way that you could.

We learned right away, within minutes, that if we had to rely on the world's view of such special children, for a great many people—more than you might think—if Trevor had been their son and they had known in advance, then he would not be here with us today. Now I must confess that when I've heard a negative comment like that, my first thoughts have been those of hurt, anger, and rejection, but what these people have really needed and what others like them will need—and that I know we'll continue to encounter in the years ahead—are our prayers, don't they? Because they're not aware of some biblical truths that, I must admit, I probably had only cursory head knowledge of before Trevor's arrival.

First, they're not aware that the Lord our God, the Lord is one. He does exist. He's the creator of the universe. He will not grow tired or weary. And while His understanding sometimes no one can fathom, He does not make mistakes, does He? No. Trevor—just like all children, even those we might think of as imperfect (just like all of us, for that matter)—is here for a reason.

Second, the world doesn't understand that "we know that in all things God works for the good of those who love Him, who have been called according to His purpose." And that does go for *all* things, doesn't it? Yes, even those things we may not have asked for.

Most importantly, however, I feel they don't understand that I know as a believer that when I die I'm going to heaven, and when I do, I'm going to lose this imperfect body and be transformed both physically and spiritually. And it is my greatest hope and prayer today—and I trust it's the same for all fathers here on this Father's Day—that our children . . . *my son* . . . will be with us there in paradise.

Now, Melissa and I have additional hopes and prayers for the Lord's wisdom and discernment in the years ahead regarding Trevor's upbringing. As a result, therefore, when we at last get to that point in heaven, although Trevor may not ever have been able to clearly articulate it in this lifetime (then again, he may lead one hundred people to Christ—God only knows), we just hope and pray that in his own glorified body he can say to us— perhaps for the first time ever in a clear, understandable voice— "Thank you, Mom and Dad, for being the kind of parents I needed you to be." And if this last month and a half is any indication (and I know it is), he's also going to be able to say, "Thank you, Voyagers Bible Church, for being the church home I needed you to be."

And yet as I stand here this morning, while I'm confident there will be many more in the years ahead, I think that the greatest blessing Melissa and I have already received from the life of our son—and it is our great desire for everyone here to also receive this morning—is something that we'll be able to tell *him* at that point in heaven. We'll be able to say, "No, Trevor, you've got it all wrong, son. Praise God . . . praise Jesus . . . and thank *you*, special boy, for the example of your life—a living, breathing, flesh-and-blood parable, teaching so many of us here so much of what we needed to know about God's perfect love. It's a love that looks at the heart, one that sees the soul inside a man and not the outward appearances—the things man looks at."

I guess because Melissa and I have that hope, we have that belief, and we do have at least that much faith, we are able to say today that while of course we certainly would not wish a disability on any of you or your families, we do appreciate all the prayers, all the support, and all the love we've received from our friends, our relatives, and this congregation. Lastly, but absolutely, positively not least, I'm here this morning to tell all of you—and more to the point perhaps, to declare to the world outside the walls of this church—that we just love our special son, Trevor William Hendershot, with all of our hearts. And with the whole earth as our witness, we *would not* have traded him for anything or with anyone in the world!

That is why we can also finally say today that while we still would not consider ourselves to be the best choice to be Trevor's parents—in fact, just the opposite—by the grace of God, with the love of our Lord and Savior Jesus Christ, and through the power of the Holy Spirit, we do consider ourselves a *family* now, most richly blessed!

Thank you all again!

1

WHAT I FEARED HAS COME UPON ME

"You probably don't remember me, but I remember you. I recognize you. I know who you are." Similar statements from strangers had startled me out of semiconscious intoxication many times before, but this time those words finally broke through the haze of my hangover on that early morning in late December of 1983. I was forced to at last acknowledge that I'd definitely become the alcoholic I'd always feared becoming; that there wasn't any person, place, or thing that could save me; and that suicide offered itself as the only possible solution to the nightmare of my miserable existence.

Robert Hendershot, alcoholic, circa 1982

1

Unfortunately, the fear that I would become an alcoholic in a family with a checkered history of drinking alcohol was actually just the first of two great fears I'd carried with me for decades. Tragically, as already indicated, that first fear is exactly what did happen.

I was born in San Diego, California, and then spent most of my childhood in the small coastal town of Newport Beach, located in Orange County, south of Los Angeles. It was a wonderful place to grow up in the '50s and '60s, with long summers spent swimming, surfing, and sailing. Yet all was not well in our dysfunctional household (though, in retrospect, we did put some fun in our dysfunctionality).

Despite the fact that I promised myself as a young boy that I would never even *touch* alcohol, I started drinking in high school as an outgrowth of my overall inability to handle life's most basic challenges. My consumption of alcohol was problematic from the first drink of beer I had at a high school party. Though I was always quiet and shy, alcohol had the immediate effect of releasing my inhibitions; suddenly, I was the outgoing and confident life of the party.

Sadly, these initial "fun" experiences while drinking quickly degenerated into out-of-control behavior and embarrassing interactions with friends, classmates, and teachers. I became known, rather infamously, as "that guy who's drunk all the time." Little did I know that my problem drinking would only get worse after I graduated from Newport Harbor High School.

I enrolled at the University of Southern California and pledged Sigma Chi fraternity. My alcohol consumption began to increase even more substantially, and I started to experience occasional blackouts (i.e., after a night of heavy drinking I would have minimal recollection of the things I had said or done the night before). Having to endure the uncertainty of not knowing with whom, where, or how I had spent several missing hours of my life was incredibly terrifying.

I also became involved in a few minor car crashes as a result of driving while under the influence of alcohol. Somehow, I was able to hold my life together enough to graduate with a BS degree.

[An important aside: It's worth noting that my alma mater's standards have improved remarkably since the 1970s. A student with my scholastic record would not even be admitted to USC today, let alone qualify to graduate with a degree. Furthermore, in recent years Sigma Chi fraternity has been a leading advocate among national fraternities in implementing alcohol awareness programs in colleges throughout the country. Although it came too late for me, Sigma Chi's Choices program (recently reconfigured and renamed Crossroads) has and will continue to be extremely helpful to undergraduate students who realize they may have problems with alcohol or other drugs.]

After graduating from USC, I moved to Costa Mesa, California, and tried to get into the real estate business, but my increasing use of alcohol, and now illegal drugs, severely limited my capacity to function in life, let alone perform satisfactorily in the workplace.

In fact, one time when I was drunk while on a surfing trip down to Mexico, I rolled a friend's car at seventy miles per hour on a narrow road a few hundred miles south of the border. My friend and I were thrown out of the car as it rolled over on top of us. The car was completely totaled, though we both miraculously survived and received only relatively minor injuries—a few cuts in my case, and my friend tore the ligaments in his knee. Fortunately, some kindly Christian missionaries were traveling north and came upon our accident and, using our surfboards as stretchers, took us back across the border in their motorhome. They tried to share some passages from the Bible with us, suggesting that maybe God had spared us for some future purpose, but I would have none of their message.

After that close call with death, the blackouts I was experiencing while drunk got worse and worse. They finally reached the point where, after a night of heavy drinking, the next morning I never knew if a concerned friend would call to see if I had made it home or an angry neighbor might knock on my door to complain about something I had said or done. Or worse, as I already alluded to at the beginning of this chapter, a stranger would stop me on the street and say something like, "You probably don't remember me, but I remember you. I recognize you. I know who you are," and then proceed to accuse me of humiliating things I had done while drunk that I had absolutely no recollection of whatsoever.

The only solution I could come up with at the time was to start drinking again immediately upon awakening. This hair-of-the-dog type of drinking not only blotted out whatever vague memories I had of the terrible things I had done while inebriated but it also mentally fortified me against any possible encounters I might have with people I had harmed the previous night. Of course, this pattern only further entrenched and escalated the vicious alcoholic cycle that had become my life. My alcoholism continued along that path for several more years.

After seriously contemplating suicide many times, finally on December 23, 1983, I cried out to God for His mercy, and He in fact did help me quit drinking *and* stay sober for the next twelve years. Over the course of those dozen years, my wife Melissa and I were married on December 23, 1985, and we prayed to receive Jesus Christ as our Lord and Savior on February 23, 1987. We were blessed with our three sons, Trevor, Taylor, and Tanner, and we moved to Irvine, California. I also switched careers and became a manufacturers' representative in the electronics industry.

My new career started out okay, but I soon fell away from the Lord, wound up in a metaphorical patch of tall weeds, and had a celebratory drink of alcohol with a customer while overseas on business in March of 1996. After having been a sober Christian for so many years, I thought I was no longer prone to alcoholism. But, unfortunately, the destructive alcoholic cycle started all over again after that first drink, proving the adage that every alcoholic faces: One drink is one too many; one thousand will never be enough.

Wedding day, December 23, 1985

My family was thoroughly exasperated by my drinking over the next eighteen months until Melissa, thankfully, finally decided she'd had enough and checked me into Hoag Hospital's Chemical Dependency Unit (CDU) in Newport Beach.

I'll never forget "coming to" in a room on the tenth floor of the CDU the next day, August 24, 1997. Waking up in an alcoholic stupor and not fully comprehending where I was, I shuffled over to the window to get my bearings. Looking out the window, off in the distance I could see the clock tower of Newport Harbor High School. The thought came to mind, *Twenty-four years since graduation. Physically, emotionally, and alcoholically, I've really come a long way, haven't I?*

Then came the awful realization that I'd thrown away my twelve years of sobriety and disgraced myself in front of my family, friends, and coworkers for over a year and a half. I seriously doubted that I'd ever be able to stop drinking again. *Oh well, I might as well jump out this window right now and save everyone the trouble of trying to fix the apparently unfixable me.*

Figuratively, if not quite yet literally, I'd already swung my right leg out the window when there was a knock on my door. "Mr. Hendershot?" a woman's pleasant voice asked.

"What?" I replied.

"It's time for breakfast."

"I'm not hungry."

"You have to eat something."

"Just slide the plate under the door."

"No, you have to come down to the dining room. We've saved a seat for you."

Clearly, this counselor wasn't going away, so I opened the door and followed her down the hall to a table where, sure enough, she had saved a seat for me. On my left sat this teenage punk rocker covered with so many tattoos and piercings that it looked like he had fallen face-first into a fishing tackle box. To my right was an older man who was shaking like a mackerel on the deck of a half-day boat.

Across from me was a woman who might have been young and pretty or maybe older and not so much. But God bless her, it was just hard to discern at that point because she had these two horribly disfiguring black eyes that gave her a flounder-like countenance. How she got them was anyone's guess. Regardless, she felt compelled to remark, "You know, Robert, you'd be kind of cute if you weren't so old, fat, and stupid."

I thought, *Well, isn't this a fine kettle of fish I've fallen into! What am I doing here?* However, by the end of that breakfast fellowship my thinking had turned completely around. *These are my people. I do need to be here. I'm just as broken as everyone else in this place.*

Retrospectively appropriating a quote I would hear many years later in a different context from Pastor Greg Laurie, I'd washed up on the shores of "a hospital for sinners, not a museum for saints."

Beginning with that first morning and then increasingly throughout my three weeks in rehab, I came to believe for the first time ever that there might be some hope for me after all. I met my first sponsor, Bill S., at the hospital, and he taught me some things about alcoholics that made us different from the general population of social drinkers. First, I learned that I had developed an actual physical allergy to alcohol. Ingesting a drink of alcohol or taking a drug triggered an uncontrollable craving in my body that compelled me so that I *had* to have one more and then another and another, ad infinitum.

Second, I learned that I had a mental obsession with the thought that *next time things will be different. I'll eventually be able to control my drinking.* I clung to that idea—even though, over and over again, the same out-of-control alcohol consumption always occurred after I had just one drink of alcohol. After so many years of suffering through this pattern of living, I found great relief in at last understanding why I had struggled with alcohol and drugs for much of my adult life. It was also very liberating to then learn that I could recover from this seemingly hopeless predicament by wholeheartedly following God's will for my life.

And what is God's will for my life—and, in fact, for everyone's life? Primarily, He wants all men to come to the knowledge of the truth and to be saved. What does it mean to be saved? Salvation occurs when, by faith, we trust Jesus Christ to forgive our sins and to provide the certain hope of eternal life with Him in heaven. From that moment on we are *justified*—free from sin's penalty regarding our past. We have set in motion the process of being *sanctified*—free from sin's power in the present. And we will one day be *glorified*—free from sin's presence in our future home in heaven.

What must I do to be saved? I must believe that Jesus Christ—fully God and fully man—died on the cross as payment for my sins and rose from the grave on the third day. I must admit that I am a sinner, agree to turn *from* sin *to* God, acknowledge Jesus as my Lord and Savior, and then accept His free gift of forgiveness, salvation, and eternal life in heaven. Reciting the following short prayer out loud will help an individual take the final, all-important step of faith: "Lord Jesus, I receive You as my Lord, God, and personal Savior. Amen."

Due to the craziness of my recent behavior, I felt it was necessary to recommit my life to the Lord while in rehab. Since that day, I've always tried to remember that I'm saved by God's mercy, not by my merit; by my trusting, not by my trying; and by Christ's dying, not by my doing.

As a recovering alcoholic, God's secondary will for my life is that I stay sober so that I might eventually emerge as the Christian man, husband, and father He would have me become. I learned that the best way to accomplish that goal was to maintain a healthy spiritual condition and follow a simple (though not easy) twelve-step program. Every week for the past twenty years, I've attended one or two twelve-step meetings, as well as two or three men's Bible studies. In addition, I've tried to take my family to church two times every week. I've also intentionally surrounded myself with other faithful Christian men—some, like me, who have needed recovery from something, along with many others who have not.

> As iron sharpens iron,
>> so one man sharpens another.

(Proverbs 27:17)

I also realize how truly fortunate I am that my family still loves, prays for, and supports me in my recovery. The sad fact is that many alcoholics like me never get the help they need, and they eventually wind up dead or in jail for a very long time. Praise be to the God and Father of our Lord Jesus Christ because it's only by His grace, mercy, and love that I have continued to remain sober, one day at a time, since August 24, 1997.

2

WHAT I DREADED HAS HAPPENED TO ME

My *second* great fear while growing up was in regard to the type of father I would be—or more importantly, how my children would turn out. After Melissa and I were married, we tried for many years to become parents—daily prayer, monthly heartbreak, and more than five years of struggling with the disappointment of infertility. When Melissa finally became pregnant, I had all these hopes and dreams that our child would be everything I never was in life: a great leader, a tremendous athlete, a skilled musician, an outstanding scholar. At the very least, I hoped that our child would be happy and content with who he or she was in life and not have to resort to alcohol or drugs in order to feel comfortable in his or her own skin.

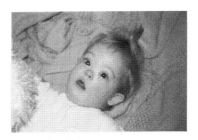

Trevor, age 1

Melissa went into labor on Friday morning, May 4, 1990, and we hurried off to the hospital. After I saw my first and most likely only child being born and heard the doctor say, "He's a boy!" that was the happiest moment of my life. But when that same doctor, five minutes later, asked me, "Do you know what Down syndrome is?" that was by far the saddest moment of my life. Let me tell you that to go from utter joy to utter devastation in the five seconds it took for the doctor to finish her question was the most painful thing I've ever had to endure. It was far worse than anything I'd ever felt after a night of drinking.

I've always compared that moment to a fast-forwarded version of the destructive cycle that all alcoholics go through in their drinking "careers." Initially, feelings of joyful elation sweep over us after consuming our first drink of alcohol because we think we've discovered a magic elixir that will make all of our problems go away and everything right in our world. But then inevitably—five, ten, or even twenty years later—come the feelings of complete despair when we realize how alcohol has turned on us and how our addiction to it has ruined our lives for all intents and purposes. I figure the only potential parallel to the emotional pain I felt when I learned that Trevor had Down syndrome would be if it were possible to compress that normally years-long sequence of alcoholic destruction into an elapsed time of about five seconds.

Like most people, I had a basic idea of what it meant to have Down syndrome. I knew, for instance, that Trevor would be physically and mentally delayed in his development. Still, nothing could have prepared me for the shock of having our son born with this disability. Thankfully, sympathetic parishioners from Voyagers Bible Church heard the news and quickly came to the hospital to help us bear this burden in any way that they could. Having our church congregation surround us with prayers, support, and love was the first sign of hope for Melissa and me that things might someday be okay with our son.

Nevertheless, I had such a sense of loss on that "not-so-Good" Friday morning that I didn't even want to bring Trevor home and told Melissa that we should just put him up for adoption. Fortunately, my beautiful wife had already fallen in love with Trevor and unreservedly welcomed him into our family. As for me, for the rest of that Friday and on through Saturday, I remained shocked, heartbroken, and even angry with God: "You knew how hard it was going to be for me to be even a halfway-decent father of a 'regular' boy, let alone one with special needs! Why did You do this to *me*, of all people? You've made a big mistake! There's no way I can raise a handicapped child. *I don't deserve a son like this!*" I cried myself to sleep that Saturday night.

*   *   *

Christians often talk about lifting someone up in prayer, but when the several hundred people from our church prayed for us over that weekend, I actually experienced that feeling for the first time. As a direct result of their prayers, I had the physically tangible sensation that God was there with us and He would carry me through my sadness. By the time I woke up the next morning—now feeling like it was truly Easter Sunday—I had also begun to more fully understand some things about God that I had little knowledge of before Trevor's birth.

First and foremost, I began to appreciate that the Lord our God is the creator of the universe, and though His ways sometimes no one can fathom, He does not make mistakes. No, Trevor, just like all children, even those whom we might see as imperfect because they have a disability—just like all of us for that matter—was here for a reason.

Second, I started to truly realize that in all things God works for the good of those who love Him, who have been called according to His purpose. And that does go for *all* things, even those we may not have asked for.

Finally, as a believer, I knew that when I died, I would go to heaven, lose my own imperfect body, and be transformed physically and spiritually. As Trevor's father, I now had the divinely given responsibility to nurture him and train him up in the way he should go so that his overall life would be one of faith and trust in God and that he would therefore spend eternity together with us in heaven.

Recalling the wisdom found in the shortened form of Reinhold Niebuhr's "Serenity Prayer" (read at every twelve-step meeting) was particularly appropriate as I anticipated moving forward in with my relationship with Trevor:

> God, grant me the serenity to accept the things I can-
>   not change,
> Courage to change the things I can,
> And wisdom to know the difference.

I realized that I couldn't change the reality of Trevor having Down syndrome, but with God's help, I could and would change my attitude about his having a disability. As a consequence, that Sunday morning, three days after Trevor's birth, I couldn't wait to get back to the hospital in order to officially welcome my beau-tiful son into our family.

Melissa, Trevor and Robert

The funny thing is that the twenty-six years since Trevor's birth, with all of their setbacks and successes, have only served to prove that I was right all along when I said, "I don't deserve a son like this." You see, while I really *did* deserve my alcoholism—I drank far too much, far too often, and for far too long—I really *did not* deserve a son like Trevor, albeit for the completely opposite reason. The balance of this book will attempt to describe how I came to that inescapable conclusion.

Angel for Higher further seeks to explain how synergizing the lessons I learned from my struggles with alcoholism together with the challenges of raising my son with Down syndrome resulted in tremendous blessings, not only in Trevor's life and mine but also in the lives of Melissa; his younger brothers, Taylor and Tanner; and the dozens of friends he makes everywhere he goes. He's also been a wonderful influence in the lives of the hundreds of classmates he's attended school with, the thousands of parishioners he's inspired at the churches we've attended, and the tens of thousands of baseball and hockey fans he's positively impacted while working at his jobs as team store greeter for both Major League Baseball's Los Angeles Angels and the National Hockey League's Anaheim Ducks. An angel for higher, if you will.

3

Become Even More
Undignified Than This

After I was released from rehab in mid-September 1997, my sponsor suggested that I should make amends to the people in my life who were negatively impacted by my actions while I was under the control of alcohol: "Fools mock at making amends for sin, but goodwill is found among the upright" (Proverbs 14:9).

I made direct amends to my family, friends, coworkers, and strangers (at least those I could remember harming) by apologizing and asking each of them what I could do to make things right.

I explained to them that this process was important to my continued sobriety. I was grateful that the response I received from most was something like, "Robert, just don't drink anymore and we're good."

Mercifully, everyone close to me seemed to be satisfied with my amends—that is, everyone except Trevor.

Frankly, while in the throes of my alcoholism, I was not always mentally, emotionally, or even physically present in the ways I had been for the first few years of his life. In addition, although he couldn't clearly express himself verbally, I could tell he was bothered by some of the words I'd said and by the hurtful actions I inflicted on him while I'd been drinking.

Trevor, age 4

I knew I had to come up with a way of making a more earnest apology to him through my actions (known in twelve-step programs as a living amends) because actions do speak louder than words.

This is where the concept I call Synergy of Suffering began to strengthen my previously feeble attempts at becoming the Christian man, husband, and father who might actually please God someday. Let me be specific.

All the boys in our house (me included) love watching videos of the Three Stooges, that slapstick trio of comics who starred in movie shorts of the black-and-white era. While all of us enjoy their face slapping, eye poking, and pie-in-the-face antics, Trevor, for some reason, especially laughs during a particular scene that occurs only now and then in the Stooges' adventures. That's when an anvil—or something equally unpleasant—lands on the foot of one of the Stooges.

Understandably, this unfortunate Stooge grabs his bad foot and hops around on the other leg, shouting "Ow! Ow! Ow!" The other two Stooges take that as a signal to commence this crazy routine: One folds his arms and kicks his legs out in a slow,

Cossack-style dance, while the other begins to clap rhythmically to the dancing Stooge's painful hopping, all the while chanting, "Hey! Hey! Hey!"

No matter how many times he sees it, Trevor always cracks up watching this absurdly madcap scene.

When Trevor started attending public school, his district would send a small, yellow school bus to pick him up at our house at seven thirty in the morning. Melissa had to be at work fairly early, so I would wait for the bus with Trevor on the sidewalk in front of our house.

After Trevor got on the bus, he and I would launch into our own version of the Three Stooges routine: Trevor would look out the bus window; give me a big smile; say, "Hey! Hey! Hey!" through the window; and start slowly clapping for me. I would fold my arms, start my own Cossack dance, and continue until his bus pulled away, turned the corner, and drove out of sight.

An interesting thing started happening in the neighborhood as a result of our routine. Whenever that bus came down the street, neighbors backing out of their driveways would slow down and adjust their rearview mirrors, teenagers on bicycles would drop something in order to have to stop to pick it up, and children walking to elementary school would just stop and stare. It seemed everyone wanted to see me make a fool of myself—but that was absolutely okay by me.

The truth was, when I thought of all the foolish things I'd done while drinking, the least I could do was act the fool for my son as part of a living amends so that he knew that his daddy was sober (it would have been problematic to dance on a sidewalk so early in the morning otherwise), loved him with all of his heart, and would not have traded him for anything or anyone in the world.

After I had been sober a couple of years, though, my life started getting better all around, and I was kind of hoping I might be able to somehow convince Trevor that we could dispense with our dancing Stooges routine. Besides, now that my work was picking up, I felt that taking time out for dancing was negatively affecting my busy mornings.

But then the vice principal of Trevor's elementary school called to tell me he was going to suspend Trevor for screaming profanity and making obscene gestures. *What?*

When I went to his office and asked him what had happened, the VP explained, "I guess Trevor felt that some kid was teasing him, so he yelled a profanity and made an obscene gesture." (Sadly, this wouldn't be the last time Trevor would be harassed by some of his classmates during his school years.)

I asked the VP, "What exactly did he say and do?"

He replied, "I'll tell you, but I'm not going to yell like Trevor did."

"Okay, fine," I said.

According to the VP, after one particular kid kept teasing him, Trevor finally had enough and yelled at the top of his lungs, "My daddy loves me! Forget you!" and flipped off the other student.

I wanted to be sure I understood what had happened. "Trevor said, 'My daddy loves me! Forget you!' and then he gave this kid the finger. That's it? Well, with all due respect, Mr. VP, while that wouldn't have been my first choice for Trevor—"

The VP interrupted, "We have zero tolerance for that type of behavior at our school!"

I replied, "I was going to say that I grew up in the '60s, and we found that a punch in the nose would usually solve problems of this sort."

To this he stated, "We'd expel Trevor for that!"

I said, "I understand. Times have changed. But I guarantee that would be the last time this kid hassled my son. In any event, since the playground volunteers seem unable to stop this bullying, how about if Trevor could come to you when this sort of stuff happens? If word gets out on the playground that you're going to get involved, I bet this would all go away. What do you think?"

The VP agreed and then said, "Mr. Hendershot, you've been very reasonable. Trevor is across the hall in the principal's office.

The day's almost over, so why don't you just take him home now? Bring him back to school tomorrow, and we'll consider this incident closed."

We shook hands, and I went across the hall to get Trevor. He was pretty despondent. I could tell he'd been crying. As we walked to our car, he whimpered, "I sorry, Daddy."

I assured him, "That's okay. I understand. I forgive you, and I know God will forgive you too. Please just try to see Mr. VP or talk to me if something like this happens again. And while I know you're sorry, there's still going to be some *very* severe consequences for saying and doing what you did."

He mumbled sorrowfully, "Okay."

I said, "I'll let you choose . . . Do you want chocolate or vanilla ice cream?"

Trevor was stunned for a moment and then said with a big smile, "Chocolate!"

"Good choice! And you probably want three scoops, right?" I asked.

"Yes!" he stated emphatically.

"All right! Me too! Let's go!"

*   *   *

I decided to keep dancing for Trevor on the sidewalk. We kept up our routine for many more years until it came time to move and we put our home up for sale. It sold after a few months.

On what would be our last morning at the house, a large moving van was idling out front when Trevor's bus came down the street. By then Taylor and Tanner had grown older and started joining me on the sidewalk. The three of us formed a Rockettes-style kickline while we all danced for Trevor. Even the bus driver clapped for us on this last day.

But the greatest blessing occurred when, although at first I couldn't see them from behind the moving van, all of our neighbors, up and down the street, had climbed out of their cars and off their bikes and were dancing for Trevor as his bus pulled away for the last time.

Trevor started at Northwood High School around the time we moved into our new home. Pursuant to his new schedule, I dropped him off and picked him up after school every day for the next four years.

After Trevor graduated from high school in 2010, he started to attend a job training/life skills transition program at Irvine Valley College. Part of his training was a requirement to learn how to ride a bus to and from his college campus. His bus stop was located at a busy, four-way stoplight intersection—and a good ten-minute walk from our home.

Trevor and I prayed about the day ahead as we made our way to the bus stop that first morning of his transition program. I also silently prayed, *Dear God, You know it's been over four years since I last put Trevor on a bus. It was one thing to dance for him in our old neighborhood where he grew up and our family lived for twenty-five years, but at this hour of the morning, there will probably be at least ten to fifteen cars filled with complete strangers either waiting at the stoplight or driving through the intersection. You know I'm well into my fifties now, was never a very good dancer to begin with, and don't want to embarrass myself in front of all these people. Could You please see to it that Trevor somehow forgets about our old dancing routine?*

Trevor hopped on the bus after it arrived a few minutes later, found an empty seat, and fastened his seat belt. Then he looked out the window, gave me his biggest smile, and started slowly clapping and saying, "Hey! Hey! Hey!" Why, of course he did!

And I started dancing this crazy Cossack dance in front of thirty or forty strangers. Of course I did!

After his bus left, I trudged home with my head down and hands deep in my pockets, preoccupied with what our new neighbors might think of us.

Halloween came a few weeks later, and Trevor and I sat on our front porch handing out candy to the trick-or-treaters. An elderly man of foreign descent was walking unsteadily on the other side of our street, but he quickly hobbled across the road to our house after he saw us sitting in our chairs. With tears in his eyes, he vigorously shook both of our hands as Trevor and I looked at each other thinking, *What's up with this guy?*

And then the man explained in heavily accented English, "Bus stop . . . bus stop . . ."

Taylor, Trevor and Tanner

4

THAT THE WORK OF GOD
MIGHT BE DISPLAYED

Who has woe? Who has sorrow?
　　Who has strife? Who has complaints?
　　Who has needless bruises? Who has bloodshot eyes?
Those who linger over wine,
　　who go to sample bowls of mixed wine.
Do not gaze at wine when it is red,
　　when it sparkles in the cup,
　　when it goes down smoothly!
In the end it bites like a snake
　　and poisons like a viper.
Your eyes will see strange sights,
　　and your mind imagine confusing things.
You will be like one sleeping on the high seas,
　　lying on top of the rigging.
"They hit me," you will say, "but I'm not hurt!
　　They beat me, but I don't feel it!
When will I wake up so I can find another drink?"

King Solomon wrote these words almost three thousand years
ago in Proverbs 23:29–35, but I could have written them
myself—especially that last question—before I got sober.

Obviously, despite the fact that Israel had the original, etched-in-stone Ten Commandments in its possession, we learn from this passage that there were some alcoholic Israelites to be found among God's chosen people.

Although some fortunate souls down through the millennia have been able to quit their dependence on alcohol, sobriety on a large scale was never achieved by any society until Bill W. and Dr. Bob, borrowing tenets from the Bible and other Christian writings, put together the program of Alcoholics Anonymous in 1935.

Untold thousands of alcoholics like me are eternally grateful that they did, because without their twelve-step program, most of us would either be dead, institutionalized, or locked up in jail for a very long time. In my case, if I'd never gotten sober, the best I could have possibly hoped for regarding my relationship with Trevor would have been for him to visit me in jail from time to time and ask, "When you come home, Daddy?"

If you think it's been tough for alcoholics over the centuries, people born with Down syndrome were, for the most part, simply exterminated soon after birth. To be sure, some of these fortunate souls did have the opportunity to live beyond the cradle by the fortuitous circumstance of having been born to parents belonging to communities of faith that valued all human life.

After all, God said to Moses, "Who gave man his mouth? Who makes him deaf or mute? Who gives him sight or makes him blind? Is it not I, the LORD?" (Exodus 4:11–12). And later, King David wrote, "For you created my inmost being; you knit me together in my mother's womb. I praise you because I am fearfully and wonderfully made; your works are wonderful, I know that full well" (Psalm 139:13–14).

Yet it wasn't until Eunice Kennedy Shriver founded the Special Olympics in 1962 that those with developmental disabilities really began to be included in the mainstream of public life.

Prior to the mid-twentieth century, if your child was born with Down syndrome, you'd actually have to go to court to get approval to bring your child home. The prevalent thinking was that children with Down syndrome would never contribute to society in any meaningful way, that they would just be a burden to all concerned, and that it would therefore be better for their families if they were put away in an institution for the rest of their lives.

If that were the case today, the best I could possibly have hoped for regarding my relationship with Trevor would have been for *me* to visit *him* in his padded cell from time to time, to hopefully help him to discern that I was his father, and then to maybe hear from him, "When I come home, Daddy?"

Christians sometimes long for "the good old days" when life was simpler, marriages typically lasted longer, and most people generally adhered to traditional Judeo-Christian values. Yet Solomon wisely cautioned, "Do not say, 'Why were the old days better than these?' For it is not wise to ask such questions" (Ecclesiastes 7:10).

While certain aspects of modern society are decidedly contrary to traditional religious beliefs, over the last several decades our culture has indeed made wonderful progress in compassionately dealing with people with disabilities, as well as understanding the processes required to help people to recover from addictions.

Regretfully, Christians have sometimes failed to take full advantage of the programs and procedures that God, through the general grace with which He blesses all mankind, has put into place to help lessen some of life's challenges and difficulties. This refusal to accept outside-the-church help reminds me of a modern parable you may have heard.

During a rising flood, a man standing on the roof of his house prayed, "God, please save me!"

Shortly thereafter, a boat came by, and the captain said, "Get into the boat!"

The man replied, "No! God will save me!"

Then a helicopter came along. Lowering a ladder, the pilot shouted, "Grab onto the ladder!"

And the man again replied, "No! God will save me!"

Finally, the flood waters rose, covered the house, and the man drowned. After his arrival in heaven, the man asked God, "Why didn't You save me?"

God replied, "Who do you think sent the boat? Who do you think sent the helicopter?"

As parents of special-needs children, we too sometimes fail to get into the boat and take advantage of the many resources available for people with disabilities. As Christians struggling with addictions, we also sometimes fail to grab onto the ladder of twelve-step programs that can help us get and stay sober and then live healthy, productive, and God-honoring lives.

*   *   *

As I've already stated, some of my life's greatest blessings have come from being able to synergize what I've learned from grabbing the ladder of recovery with getting into the boat of people with disabilities. Synergistically blending the lessons gained from dealing with these two challenges has culminated in tremendous blessings to our family and to some other families as well. Let me share another example.

After I had been sober a few years, the parents of the players on Trevor's Irvine Sharks AYSO VIP soccer team came to me and asked if I could take over for the current coach who was moving away. I didn't know anything about coaching, even less about soccer, but I did know quite a bit about being the parent of a child with a disability. So I took the position. I knew that these children, along with their parents, often felt ostracized by the general population as they went about their daily lives.

Therefore, I wanted to make sure our practices and games were safe places where their children would feel welcomed for the very quirks and behaviors that were perhaps frowned upon everywhere else they went. This concept was learned from people in recovery: As reprehensible, antisocial, and in many cases, as illegal as some of their earlier actions had been, these very actions had "bought them a ticket" into twelve-step recovery groups where they could enjoy fellowship and feel welcomed by those in similar predicaments.

So we started our first soccer practice, and every practice thereafter, by having every player and their parents sit down in a large circle on the grass. We would then go around the circle, and everyone—parents as well as players—would introduce themselves so that we could all meet one another and be recognized as part of the team. We wanted to assure them that we were all in this together and that, as members of the team, they were part of a community of families with disabilities. Most twelve-step meetings also begin in a similar way: systematically, sequentially, we introduce ourselves with something like, "Bob H., alcoholic," until everyone present has confirmed that they are indeed qualified to be there.

Some of our players were not as athletically skilled as others, and they tended to wander mentally and physically. So we made our practices and games audience-participation events. Parents, siblings, and friends (we called all of them "buddies") were invited out onto the field to hold their player's hand and then gently lead him or her around the field in order to help the player participate, enjoy some much-needed exercise, and hopefully feel more like a part of the team. As a result, at any one point in time, we might have thirty to forty people running around on the field. Any resemblance between our practice of soccer and more traditional games was purely coincidental!

This concept also had its origins in recovery groups. When many of us alcoholics who are in the initial stages of recovery—and even well beyond—encounter struggles with life, we need the help of someone with more experience and longer sobriety to help us navigate the uncharted waters of living life without the crutch of using alcohol or drugs. Some of the simplest day-to-day challenges that were previously troublesome are easier when we have a mentor (or in twelve-step program lingo, a sponsor) to give us direction.

In the past, we "sponsees" (as we're called) dealt with many of our issues by drinking, which of course only made things worse. But now our sponsor could—based on his or her own experience—make suggestions to help guide us when life is "in session." Sometimes sponsors do have to figuratively drag their sponsees around the field of their often chaotic lives for many years.

* * *

That first season on our team, we had a just-stands-there player whom I'll call Sam. Although his mother brought him to every practice and every game, I wasn't even sure Sam knew there was a game going on, let alone how to play soccer. The whole season he didn't say or do much of anything other than stand there with a pleasant smile on his face. For some reason, Sam's mom was always reluctant to come out onto the field, and so for the last game of the season, I nominated myself to be Sam's buddy/sponsor. Once again I showed him the ball and how to kick it, but he gave no indication that I was even on his radar.

I had to hurry off to start the game because I was also the referee. But before leaving, I pulled Sam over to our opponents' goal and told him to just stand there the whole game, face the goal, and kick the ball if he saw it coming. As it turned out, the ball did happen to roll in front of Sam, and amazingly, he reared back and absolutely crushed the ball into the back of the net! His mother jumped about five feet in the air as Sam ran around the field shouting, "Goal! Goal! Goal!" Now I couldn't keep him quiet!

* * *

After a few years, I turned the coaching over to another parent. By then we had between twenty-five and thirty players competing on three different skill-level teams, and I'd been made commissioner of the league. But the most rewarding moments of the time I spent in the world of soccer occurred after the last game of every season.

We didn't have a Gatorade bucket, nor could the players have lifted one if we had. Instead, as an end-of-season ritual, the players chased me around the soccer field, tackled me, and then dog-piled on top of me. Could it get any better for a hope-less, helpless recovering alcoholic like me than to have fifteen babbling and slobbering soccer players with autism, cerebral palsy, and Down syndrome climbing all over me and saying, "We love you, Coach Bob"?

Irvine Sharks AYSO VIP soccer team

5

IN ALL THINGS GOD WORKS
FOR THE GOOD

When facing a crisis, the purpose of which seems to make no logical sense to me, I've always been drawn back to the verse from Paul's letter to the Romans: "And we know that in all things God works for the good of those who love Him, who have been called according to His purpose" (Romans 8:28).

Meditating on this verse influences me to stop asking God, "Why has this happened to me?" Instead, I'm prompted to ask, "Now that this has happened, God, what would You have me do?"

This question reminds me that God chooses the challenges we go through, but we choose how we go through them. He's more concerned with developing my character than in making me comfortable. He's more interested in nurturing my long-term holiness than my short-term happiness.

This perspective has been particularly helpful in raising Trevor. For instance, he's always hated shots and anything having to do with needles. He's better with those types of procedures now, but shots at the doctor's office used to be a source of tremendous grief to everyone involved. I'll never forget one time when he was about twelve years old.

Melissa and I had to take him to get his blood drawn at a laboratory for some standard medical tests. We made sure to arrive before the lab opened in order to be first in line, get it over with quickly, and—we hoped—minimize the emotional and physical pain of the whole experience. On the way to the lab, Trevor kept asking, "No shot?!?" We could (somewhat) honestly reply, "No, you're not getting a shot." After all, he was just getting blood drawn, so we were technically telling the truth, right? Well . . .

In any event, we were glad to discover that we would be the first in line that morning. But when the nurse came out and ushered us into the examination room, Trevor really started to panic. Then the nurse had a lot of trouble trying to find a vein due to Trevor's low muscle tone. He started crying, "I sorry, Daddy! I'll be good! I promise!" He thought he was being punished for something.

Hearing the commotion, another nurse came into our room, but she didn't have much luck either. By now Trevor was really screaming, refusing to sit still, and waving his arms around.

That's when a large, angry nurse came in from a back room and shouted, "What's going on here?" Now I was scared too! She ordered Trevor to lie down on the gurney, Melissa to hold his right arm, and me to pin him down like in a wrestling match.

So there we were, struggling to hold our crying son still as the nurse plunged the needle into his arm again and again, trying to find a vein. I'll never forget the look of terror on Trevor's face, just inches away from mine. The fear in his eyes seemed to say, "How could *you*, of all people, the one I've loved and trusted for all these years—why would *you* put me through this undeserved pain?" Trevor wasn't able to comprehend that we were doing this to make sure he was healthy. At last Angry Nurse finally found a vein and drew Trevor's blood. After more than forty-five minutes, the procedure was mercifully over.

We slogged out into the waiting area and discovered that the whole room was packed with adults and children. Most of them were staring and wondering, *What was going on back there?* Younger children, no doubt anxious before they arrived, now were really frightened and clinging to their mothers.

Surveying this scene and hoping there was some way we could calm their fears, I turned to Trevor and asked him in a loud voice, "Now, Trevor, that wasn't so bad, was it?"

He looked at me, paused, turned to the crowd, and yelled, "There's a bad lady back there! Run for your lives!"

With that, he bolted out the front door, and pandemonium prevailed throughout the lab—little children sobbing, mothers trying to comfort them, fathers angrily glaring at us. I told Melissa, "Sign us out. I have to stop Trevor before he runs out into the street and gets hit by a car!"

I caught him at the edge of the parking lot, and Melissa came out shortly thereafter. When I asked her if everything was okay in the lab, she said, "I'm sure ten years from now this morning will just be a painful, decade-old memory for everyone." Not too reassuring. Anyway, we were done and out of there! Whew!

* * *

I recall not liking shots also when I was a young boy—still don't. I remember trying to convince my parents to let me skip the obligatory polio vaccine of the early '60s: "Please don't make me get the shot! I promise I won't get polio!" They still took me to get the shot despite my protestations. Why? Simply because they had my best interests at heart.

And now fifty-five years later, I'm glad they did, because the threat of polio was a very real danger at the time, and my parents knew this immunization was a reasonable precaution. As a five-year-old, though, with my limited understanding, I thought that a polio shot was a painfully unnecessary procedure, while it really was a decision made by parents who were concerned about my long-term well-being.

So what's the lesson I've learned from all this? It's what I've tried to remember during those times in my life when I've found myself in situations I thought I didn't deserve—and not just those occasions related to my alcoholism or Trevor's disability. When feeling unjustly (in my opinion) singled out and struggling to understand why God has allowed a certain predicament into my life, it would be easy to complain to God, "How could You do this to me? You, of all people! I've trusted You with my life, and now You let this to happen to me!"

And that's when I try to remember that while God doesn't tell us not to *try* to understand, He does tell us not to *lean* on our understanding. After all, He reminds us, His ways are not our ways, and His thoughts are not our thoughts. That being the case, we need to remember to continually trust Him by faith and that all His reasons will eventually be revealed to us. And if those reasons are not revealed to us in this lifetime, then maybe God will offer an explanation in the next lifetime where we'll have all eternity to discuss these perceived injustices with Him.

But I'm going to assume that looking back from the perspective of infinite eternity on the sum total of the suffering we experienced during our years on this earth will be like looking back on that five-second polio shot from the perspective of fifty-five years later. I think our questions will by then have either faded away or been transformed from "Why me, God?" to "Why *not* me, God?"

I also believe that we'll ultimately be able to say to Him, "Thank You, God." For no matter how many years of pain some of us may have endured in this lifetime—and I know full well that many have suffered through far, far worse circumstances than I've ever experienced—if we've nevertheless trusted in God with all of our hearts, we'll be counted among the Christians of whom could be said, "Blessed is the man who perseveres under trial, because when he has stood the test, he will receive the crown of life that God has promised to those who love Him" (James 1:12).

6

MAKE A JOYFUL NOISE
UNTO THE LORD

Trevor has always seemed to be more in tune with God than most Christians, even from his earliest years. Well, at least far more than I've been, although that's certainly not the highest of standards. I'm not saying that Trevor has always been a perfect angel, but rather that he does seem able to see beyond the physical world and to have insights into the spiritual world that the rest of us can only imagine.

I remember once when he was probably five or six years old, Melissa and I put him into a time-out in our downstairs bathroom for some minor transgression. Very angry about his punishment, he slammed the door behind him and started to complain loudly about "stupid Mommy" and "dumb Daddy." Melissa and I stood outside the room, trying not to laugh.

After he quieted down and hadn't said anything for a few minutes, we leaned in close to the door to try to hear what he was doing. That's when we heard him say in a clear voice, "Okay, God, I hear You. I sorry, God. I say sorry to Mommy and Daddy."

Then he came out and sheepishly apologized, "I sorry, Mommy and Daddy. I do better. Please forgive?"

I said, "That's okay, Trevor. We forgive you, and maybe we

were too hard on you." Melissa and I were kind of hoping Trevor wouldn't call down fire from heaven on the both of us!

*   *   *

As he grew older, Trevor began to express his love for God by standing up at church, raising his arms, and singing loudly during worship. We used to be concerned by what others might think of his off-key singing, but it just caused a bigger scene whenever we tried to get him to turn his volume down, let alone trying to have him sit in his seat.

As a way to avoid any disturbance, we always try to sit in the same seats at church every week so that those who choose to sit near us know in advance what they'll be hearing in the way of an a cappella and off-beat, though certainly heartfelt, vocal concert from Trevor.

In addition to actively participating in our church's Sunday morning worship services, Trevor always wanted to go on a men's retreat like the ones I had attended. I was reluctant to take him due to some of his unusual quirks that I feared might disrupt the spiritual purpose of a retreat. Basically, I was worried that men who had invested their valuable time and hard-earned money in order to experience time alone with God and other men might be distracted by some of Trevor's behaviors. He never did anything too unusual (that is, for someone with a disability), but—truth be told—I was concerned that something could go wrong during the retreat and he might embarrass me in front of everyone.

I prayed at length about the next upcoming retreat and, with serious misgivings, signed up the both of us. When we got to the retreat center just outside of Julian, California, there were over one hundred men there, most of whom we already knew through church but also quite a few who had never met Trevor. We checked in on Friday afternoon and enjoyed an uneventful dinner in the dining hall that night. I did notice the seats around us were mostly vacant, but that was just as well because I was kind of hoping for the grace of some isolation.

After dinner, we all attended a teaching session in the enclosed amphitheater on the retreat grounds. The visiting pastor taught from under a spotlight aimed at the front of the stage, and we all sat in the surrounding tiers.

Trevor and I had no real difficulties during the Friday night or Saturday morning sessions, but the Saturday night session proved very eventful.

The session that night consisted mostly of an open-mike style program in the amphitheater. The emcee of the retreat invited any man who had a prayer request to come down to the stage and share about whatever challenge he was going through so that the rest of us could pray for God's will in his life and a resolution to his problem. Usually these prayer requests would cover health concerns, marriage difficulties, wayward children, job searches, or other issues that many men face at some point in life.

As Trevor and I sat in the front row listening to the men share, he kept bugging me, "You share, Daddy." But I wasn't really feeling it.

Finally, though, due to his persistent urging, I got up, walked across the stage, and accepted the microphone from the emcee.

I shared about how I had struggled with alcoholism for years but was now working a twelve-step program and at that point had been sober for about eleven years. A few of the men already knew this about me because they had heard me share my testimony in front of the entire church a few years earlier. Unable to see anyone in the audience because of the semi-blinding spotlight shining down on me, I could only imagine what the other men were thinking.

I also shared about what it was like raising my son Trevor and some of the things that God had taught me through his life. I mentioned that it always seemed so *interesting* to me that Trevor might live out his life simply, innocently, and unpretentiously but full to the brim with God's love, and yet the world seemed to think he was lacking in many ways. But did God see Trevor that way? I didn't think so.

It had always seemed so *ironic* to me that God, who spoke a Word and the universe leapt into existence, chose to create Trevor—and every other individual with Trisomy 21 Down syndrome—by placing forty-seven chromosomes in each and every one of his cells, while the rest of us have but forty-six (twenty-three each from our mother and father).

Let me put it differently. Our omniscient, omnipotent, and omnipresent God knew full well in advance that mankind would one day develop the technological capabilities to land men on the moon, manufacture high-speed computers, and achieve medical breakthroughs such as the ability to recognize chromosomes as microscopic building blocks of life. At the same time, He also knew full well that mankind would then put an inordinate value on the material things and the fast-paced lifestyle that these various technologies offered.

Yet despite knowing all this, He still chose to use an additional forty-seventh chromosome, an extra byte of coded genetic information, in each and every one of Trevor's cells to give him his special and unique characteristics.

According to the world's view, though, forty-five or even forty-four chromosomes would've probably made more sense because most people see individuals with Down syndrome as "less than" the rest of us, and so they couldn't possibly be operating with a complete set of chromosomes.

So, I wondered, *might God be trying to tell us something?* Perhaps, for instance, that He considers people with Down syndrome to be new and improved versions of us "normal" humans. Maybe He intentionally placed extra chromosomes in the cells of people with Down syndrome as signposts for us to discover in this age of modern technologies. Maybe He was hoping that as a result we might appreciate what He considers to be mankind's most valuable qualities, i.e., that in God's eyes people with Down syndrome are really upgrades from typical humans, that they're the ones who most closely follow after God's own heart.

I finished my testimony by declaring that it always seemed so *wonderful* to me that Jesus, while He walked on earth, took time out from His busy schedule to observe the simple, innocent, and unpretentious faith of little children and then comment, "The kingdom of heaven belongs to such as these." I handed the microphone back to the emcee and started to return to my seat. However, to my great surprise, Trevor hurried past me in order to grab the microphone from the emcee.

More than a little alarmed, I asked him loudly, "Trevor, what are you doing?"

"Now we sing!" he exclaimed.

"No, you can't sing now! It's not time for singing!" I protested, but it was too late. The emcee had already handed the microphone to Trevor.

I tried to take it from him, but he turned his back on me and launched into one of the loudest, most unintelligible versions of "Be Thou My Vision" ever heard on earth.

When I tried to pull the microphone out of his hands, Trevor just turned away and kept shuffling across the stage with his back to me, singing all the while. I tried to stop him, but there was nothing I could do short of tackling him and wrestling him to the stage.

Trevor's singing lasted for five excruciatingly painful minutes. Finally, after mercifully finishing the last verse, he handed the microphone back to the emcee, and we both slunk back to our seats—all to complete silence from the rest of the men.

Aware of how upset I was, Trevor said quietly, "I sorry, Daddy."

With gritted teeth, I told him under my breath, "Why did you do that? That was totally the wrong thing to do!" Thankfully, the emcee announced that the night's session had ended and that we would meet again in the morning for breakfast. We remained in our front-row seats—Trevor crying, me seething—as the rest of the men quietly filed out of the amphitheater.

I was so angry with Trevor! I told him later that night, "I *knew* something like this would happen if we came to the retreat—that you'd do something foolish—and that's exactly what you did!" I barely slept that night, knowing that I'd been exposed as a rotten father who couldn't control his disabled son.

I got up early the next morning so we could pack and leave before we'd have to face the rest of the men. I woke Trevor up, told him to get ready, that we were leaving and would get breakfast on the way home. I got our suitcase, slammed the cabin door behind me, and started rolling across the parking lot to our car about seventy-five yards away.

I had just made it out of the cabin when I ran into two men from the retreat who were returning to their cabin with early morning coffee. They saw my suitcase and asked, "Where are you going? Checkout's not until noon."

I replied, "Please ask everyone to forgive Trevor and me for the disorder we caused last night. I'm so very, very sorry. We're just going to head home early this morning."

Unbelievably, one of them asked, "What are you talking about? Everyone was so touched by both of you."

"Naah, I don't think so. The amphitheater was completely quiet afterward, and everyone left so quickly."

The other man explained, "That's because there wasn't a dry eye in the house. I think everyone was afraid they'd lose it if they didn't head back to their cabins!"

The first guy insisted, "Go ahead and put your suitcase in your car, but don't go home yet. Come to breakfast, and you'll see what I mean!"

I kept walking toward my car and ran into three more men who had been at the amphitheater. One of them asked, "Where are you going?"

"Well, I felt so bad about last night that Trevor and I have already packed, and we were going to leave before breakfast."

The same guy asked, "What are you talking about?"

Another said, "You two were the best part of the night! On the way back to our cabins last night, everyone shared that they all wished that they had a song in their hearts like Trevor, that regardless of how bad their voices might sound, they'd continue to offer praise to the Lord no matter who tried to stop them."

The third guy joked, "Yeah, even if they also had a clueless dad."

I'd just reached my car when one of our pastors came up to me and said, "I've been meaning to tell you something for years but kept forgetting until I was reminded by your sharing last night. Remember when you shared your testimony at church a few years ago? Well, my mother just happened to be in the audience that day. Like you, she had struggled with alcoholism for many years. After hearing about your recovery that morning, she was encouraged to seek help. She entered into treatment and has been sober ever since that day. Sorry it's taken so long, but I want to thank you for helping to restore our family."

I decided maybe Trevor and I might stay for breakfast after all.

*   *   *

Our table was packed at breakfast. After that morning's final session ended, the retreat's organizer took the microphone to share his closing thoughts: "I've been facilitating these retreats for over twenty years, and I've always taken home some biblical insight I've learned to share with my wife and daughters. As it happened, before this retreat, my wife made a simple request: 'Maybe this year, instead of bringing home some bit of knowledge you've learned, why don't you try to find someone inspiring at the retreat, a particular person with a great passion for the Lord you could tell us about.'

"Well, let me think who that might be," he said with a grin. "I've also heard Trevor's birthday is tomorrow. And because turnabout is fair play, why don't we all sing to Trevor? I think 'Happy Birthday' will work."

All the men then stood up, sang "Happy Birthday" to Trevor, and gave him a standing ovation.

We've gone to a few more retreats since then, and Trevor always seems to touch the men who attend in a special and unique way.

I remember before one retreat the registrar pulled me aside

to ask, "I see that you and Trevor haven't signed up yet. You are coming, aren't you?"

I replied, "I'm kind of busy at work right now, and I don't think we'll be able to make it this year."

He said, "Well, Mr. Too Busy Dad, how about if I come by your house on Friday afternoon, pick Trevor up, take him to the retreat, and then bring him back home on Sunday? Would that fit into your busy schedule?"

Trevor and I both went to the retreat.

*   *   *

I've also taken Trevor to my twelve-step program birthday meetings during which members receive a chip medallion for reaching the milestone of another year of sobriety. Those whose birthdays are being celebrated at the meeting get a few minutes to share about what's been going on in their lives over the past year.

Every year after I share my story, Trevor and I repeat our Three Stooges dancing routine to the rhythmic clapping from many in the room. Recovering alcoholics naturally connect with Trevor, and my theory is that they see in him someone who, like them, struggles with life and who, like them, sometimes says or does stuff that may not fit in with societal norms. (In Trevor's case, he really can't help himself—most of the time anyway.)

They seem to appreciate the undeniably cheerful optimism he displays despite his obvious challenges. Furthermore, he hasn't had to work a twelve-step program in order to be grateful for what God has done for him.

In fact, after a birthday meeting one year, a regular member came up to me and said, "This is an open meeting, anyone can attend. And everybody loves Trevor. So you should bring him to the meetings more often."

I told him, "Well, he's not really an alcoholic, and there usually aren't enough chairs as it is. So I'd hate to have Trevor sit in the chair of someone who definitely needs to be here."

This man replied, "Well, doofus, if it's a seat you're worried about, why don't you just drop Trevor off and then go sit out in the parking lot until the meeting ends? That'd be a win-win for everybody!"

Wasn't that nice?

I realized long ago that at best, I'm just called to be Trevor's chauffeur and roadie on his journey through life.

7

A MAN AFTER GOD'S OWN HEART

After Trevor started his freshman year at Northwood High School in Irvine, we found out that he was being bullied by some students, not only because of his disability but also due to his habit of loudly singing Christian songs before school, during lunch, and in the hallways after classes were over. Imagine Trevor doing that!

I called the school's vice principal and left a voice mail expressing our concerns, identifying the bullies, and requesting that the school intervene immediately.

When the vice principal returned my call the next day, she said that she had interviewed the "alleged perpetrators" and that they had denied everything. She also stated that she tried to interview Trevor, but he seemed afraid to say anything—and she couldn't understand him even when he did manage to mumble a few words. Her bottom line was that she didn't want a "miscarriage of justice to harm the innocent students," and so in her opinion, the case was closed.

I didn't agree with her conclusion and asked to meet with her as soon as possible. She told me to come in the next day at 8:00 a.m.

The next morning, I was ushered into a meeting room where the principal, all three vice principals, four teachers, and a police officer were present. (What, no custodian?) The group was a little intimidating, but I'd brought along a surprise witness: Trevor!

Knowing that he might be fearful in such a situation, Melissa had Trevor write down what was said and what had happened to him. She wisely figured that it would be easier for Trevor to read something at the meeting rather than having to respond to questions that he may not have anticipated.

I flatly stated at the start of the meeting that this was not a deposition, that there would be no cross-examination of Trevor, and that after he read his notes, we would leave it up to the group to decide whether to take any additional action.

I asked Trevor to please start reading, and he said, "I scared, Daddy."

I reassured him that I was right there with him and encouraged him to go ahead and read because he was safe with me there.

He haltingly read, "They call me 'tarded, 'tupid, ugly, wurtless, hate you. Grabbed my neck . . . push me down . . . pour water on me."

You could have heard a pin drop after Trevor finished reading his brief soliloquy.

As we got up to leave, I told everyone, "Now you all get to decide where any miscarriage of justice might lie."

We left the meeting having acted according to a maxim I'd heard in a twelve-step meeting: Hope for the best, prepare for the worst, leave the results up to God, and you'll never be disappointed.

There was a fairly large crowd of students outside waiting to cheer for Trevor. The school's cheerleaders had even made a huge banner that said, "We love you, Trevor! You're awesome! You're the bomb!" He still has the banner.

A tackle on the varsity football team pulled aside one of the bullies and told him, "If you even say so much as 'hello' to Trevor over the next four years, I'm going to kick your behind all the way to Riverside and back."

A postscript: The bullies were suspended and kicked off their respective athletic teams. One ended up transferring to another school.

* * *

When we got home, I told Trevor, "Great job today! And that was pretty cool, getting that banner from the cheerleaders!"

He said, "I marry them!"

"Which one?"

"All of them!" he replied.

"Well," I answered, "you can't marry all of them. Besides, your mom and I have been praying for the very special young lady God has already chosen for you. We know He will bring you two together according to His timing and His good, pleasing, and perfect will."

* * *

At the start of Trevor's final year in high school, the parents of every senior received an email explaining that if they wanted their son or daughter to apply to be on the homecoming court, they would have to fill out the attached five-part document and return it to the activities office no later than noon of the following Friday. The five princes and five princesses of the homecoming court would be selected from the returned applications and announced on Tuesday. The student body would vote for the homecoming king and queen out of those ten candidates on Wednesday. The king would be announced at the noon pep rally on Friday, and the queen would be crowned during halftime of the football game that night.

I think I've filled out loan documents that were less extensive than this application! Seriously, check it out: Part one required a listing of leadership roles—class offices held, club officer positions, etc. Part two focused on athletics—sports participated in, teams played on, seasons selected to be captain, etc. Part three inquired about performing arts endeavors—plays acted in, involvement in orchestras, etc. Part four requested a listing of academic achievements—GPA, honors classes, etc. Finally, part five asked the candidate to submit a one-hundred-word essay describing their greatest contribution to Northwood High School.

I thought back to the hopes and dreams I'd had for our son before he was born. While I knew he'd made some friends at the school over the years, I also knew that this opportunity was not for Trevor and deleted the document.

Surprisingly, one of Trevor's special education teachers called Melissa later that day and asked if Trevor had turned in his application for the homecoming court. Melissa said, "We really didn't consider doing that. Frankly, Trevor hasn't achieved anything close to the application's requirements. Plus it's hard enough for him to just write his name, let alone a one-hundred-word essay." Then the teacher asked if it would be okay if he went ahead and filled out the application and turned it in for Trevor. Melissa responded, "I guess so. Whatever. Go ahead."

*　*　*

That Tuesday afternoon, I drove over to pick up Trevor after school. He came skipping across the parking lot to my car with a red rose in his hand. "Where'd you get the cool rose?" I asked.

"I on homecoming court," he replied.

In his innocence, Trevor frequently misinterprets the words and actions of others. Figuring this was one of those occasions, I said, "Trevor, I just think some nice person gave you a rose, you heard talk of the homecoming court, and you mistakenly put the two together."

He insisted, "No, Daddy! I on the homecoming court! See?" He then pulled a paper out of his backpack and handed it to me.

I looked at the document with disbelief, but sure enough it said, "Congratulations! Trevor Hendershot has been selected as one of five candidates for homecoming king for Northwood High School."

Stunned, I told Trevor, "Okay, son, I guess you're on the homecoming court!"

I wondered how this could have happened. When we got home, I asked his brothers who the other four candidates were, and they were exactly the kind of athletes, scholars, and leaders solicited by the application.

So over the next two days, I explained to Trevor what a great honor it was just to have been picked to be on the court. I also talked about the fact that the other boys were very well qualified too. I repeatedly made the request that he not get too upset if someone else was chosen as homecoming king.

*   *   *

That Friday, the entire student body gathered in the gym for the pep rally. There were hundreds of students, teachers, and administrators. The band was playing fight songs. The cheerleaders were exhorting the football players to victory. Near the end of the rally when the time came for the homecoming king to be announced, the emcee said, "Northwood High School's 2009 homecoming king is Trevor—" and he didn't even get to our last name before the whole gym erupted into a long and tearful standing ovation.

Later at home that afternoon while I was buttoning up Trevor's first tuxedo, he asked me, "I kiss the bride?"

"Son, you're homecoming king! You're not getting married! There's not going to be any kissing required in this ceremony! In fact, if you feel any specific urges while you're standing on stage with the queen, please just keep your hands in your pockets!"

*   *   *

At halftime of the game that night, the whole stadium seemed to cheer for Trevor when he walked in with a princess on his arm. After the queen was crowned, she and Trevor stood on the reviewing stand and everyone with a camera came out of the bleachers to take a picture of them. With dozens of cameras flashing, I figured that Trevor had more photographs taken of him in those fifteen minutes than I've had taken of me in my entire lifetime.

Later that night, one of the vice principals pulled me aside to say, "As you well know, some of Trevor's less tolerant classmates bullied him at the start of his freshman year. It appears their issues with Trevor were not only that he had a disability but also with his disruptive habit of loudly singing Christian hymns before, during, and after school. Of course, with your measured input we stopped the bullying, but the faculty's efforts over the years to get Trevor to curtail his singing have had little, if any, effect.

"But the truth is that over the last four years, I think this whole school has come to realize that this young man's faith is part of who he is and which, in addition to his off-key singing, always comes with a warm smile, friendly hello, fist bump, high five, or maybe even a hug for those lucky enough to have crossed his path during their day at school. So even though you and Melissa were not planning on filling out his application, the faculty of this school decided to go ahead and complete his form anyway. We knew he was fairly popular and that, if nothing else, drafting him onto the homecoming court would be a nice gesture.

"Well, little did we know that the final tally of the votes wasn't even going to be close. Trevor got more votes than the other four candidates combined—no doubt the greatest landslide in our school's history. We'd also heard rumors that we might have a riot on our hands if Trevor wasn't selected, and so it was a tremendous pleasure to have him crowned as our well-deserving homecoming king!"

After the game ended, I was grateful to have the opportunity to thank so many in the faculty for the overwhelmingly wonderful experiences Trevor had enjoyed while attending Northwood High School.

*　　*　　*

During our drive home after the game, Trevor asked, "You proud of me, Daddy?"

Saddened that he even had to ask such a question, I replied, "Trevor, I'm so very proud of the wonderful young man you have become. And this despite your having to overcome the many mistakes I've made as your father. I'm just so very sorry that I haven't always been the daddy you deserved. But even more important than what I think, I know that God is even more proud of you! And I know that someday you'll hear from Him, 'Well done, good and faithful servant! You've been faithful with one talent; I will put you in charge of many things. Come now and share your Master's happiness!'"

And what, in my opinion, is Trevor's one main talent? We all have it, though not many of us use it. I probably use it less than most. It's the talent St. Francis of Assisi spoke of when he said, "Wherever you go, preach the gospel. If necessary, use words."

Trevor's words may indeed be few, but I don't think that anyone who's had the pleasure of meeting him could deny the example of his life: a living, breathing, flesh-and-blood parable showing so many of us not only how to preach the gospel by the way we live but also by teaching so many of us so much of what we've needed to know about God's perfect love—a love that looks at the heart and sees the soul inside a person and not the outward appearances, the things that man looks at.

Northwood High School's 2009 homecoming king and queen

8

FEARFULLY AND
WONDERFULLY MADE

Through the years, in addition to AYSO VIP soccer, Trevor has enjoyed participating in Special Olympics basketball, S4EA floor hockey, and Pop Warner's Challenger flag football programs, all of which are designed for people with disabilities. Organized sports like these are wonderful opportunities for everyone involved.

- The athletes themselves benefit from much-needed physical activity, the excitement of playing in the contests, and the sense of unity that comes from being on a team.

- The athletes' families have safe environments that engage and stimulate their children. This gives these caretakers a welcome respite from day-to-day duties.

- The volunteers who help facilitate these sports are beneficiaries of the joy that can only come through helping someone who appears less fortunate than themselves.

- Finally, the spectators who attend these events are blessed from observing a beautiful slice of humanity that is mostly invisible to the general population.

However, I think that the greatest blessing that everyone involved in activities for the disabled can receive is one of a tremendously spiritual nature. I'll explain more about that at the end of this chapter.

First, some background information about what I believe is the main challenge facing the disabled sports community. Simply put, there's always a shortage of teams, coaches, volunteers, and of course, funds. Consequently, not every special athlete has an opportunity to play on a team suitable for both their age and skill level.

As a result of the limited number of teams, any given squad may have a wide range of skills and abilities. Moreover, that also means that teams frequently encounter mismatches when paired against other teams at the various tournaments held throughout the United States.

I well remember a basketball game Trevor played in several years ago. Our opponent that day was really good! A couple of their players were over six feet tall and relatively accurate three-point shooters.

Trevor's team, the Irvine Eagles, was losing by something like twenty-five to zero as the first half was ending. Trevor, the tallest player on his squad at five feet, six inches, was getting increasingly frustrated as the game wore on and, much to my dismay, ended up "losing it" before halftime.

Looking back, I suppose my greatest mistake in preparing Trevor for this game occurred the night before when we watched the WWII movie *Patton*, the one in which George C. Scott won an Academy Award for his portrayal of General Patton.

I thought the battle scenes in the movie might inspire Trevor to compete with courage and determination in the next day's game. I didn't anticipate the full ramifications of the one scene in the movie in which German planes kept strafing helpless American soldiers who were hiding behind walls and under tables.

General Patton eventually got fed up with the merciless assault, jumped up, and shouted, "All right, that's enough!"

Then he ran out into the street and started firing his pistol at the planes as they flew overhead. Those actions would appear foolhardy to most, but the Germans flew away shortly thereafter.

Unfortunately, I learned at the basketball game just how much Trevor found himself to be a spirit in kindred with the general.

To wit, as the clock wound down at the end of the first half, Trevor shouted, "All right, that's enough!" Then he ran toward the other team's best player, who was dribbling the ball down the court, and tackled him onto the hardwood floor.

Trevor jumped up, pointed at me in the stands, and shouted, "I got him, Daddy!"

For my part, I looked around with feigned innocence, as if trying to locate the despicable parent in the crowd who would encourage his son to commit such a flagrant foul.

A bench-clearing brawl would probably have occurred if this had happened anywhere but the Special Olympics. In this situation, however, the other player was awarded a couple of well-deserved free throws, he and Trevor hugged it out, and all was good.

I guess Trevor did make his point, though, because the other coach put in his second- and third-string teams in the second half, leading to a somewhat more respectable final score.

Trevor played his second season with the Saddleback Valley Wolverines Challenger flag football team in the fall of 2011. Like Special Olympics basketball, there were frequently great disparities in age and size between some of the football players.

One team we played had a couple of players well over six feet tall and three hundred pounds. Yes, they were gentle giants, but they could still cause grief if they happened to fall on anyone.

Another team had the nicest players and coaches—though their gang tattoos were initially somewhat off-putting.

We played another team at their field, which was located in the general vicinity of a penitentiary. As we drove into the parking lot, the dad carpooling with me quipped, "Are we playing the guards or the prisoners?"

Nevertheless, Trevor threw seventeen touchdown passes as quarterback and got to play for the Orange County all-star team that season.

The OC Quakes traveled to Florida that December, spent a week at Disney World, and played a Pop Warner Challenger team from North Carolina. All of the Quakes and their accompanying entourage had a great time in Florida and handled the NC team fairly easily during the football game.

Orange County Quakes 2011 Florida trip

For everyone traveling from Orange County, though, the high point of the Florida trip had to be the Pop Warner national cheerleading competition that was held in the five-thousand-seat ESPN Field House. There must have been over thirty teams from all across the United States, each composed of around twenty "typical" teenage girls.

They'd obviously been practicing their cartwheels, coordinated backflips, and human pyramids for months, and the girls themselves had perfectly matched outfits, hair, and makeup. After each performance, loud cheering echoed down from whatever section of the Field House each team's respective parents were sitting in—an unbelievably raucous atmosphere!

Then near the end of the competition, the announcer said, "As our final contestants, we have a special team from Orange County, California. Let's hear it for the O.C. Quakes!"

The dull roar of the crowd faded to complete silence as our special-ability girls ambled out onto the stage. No cartwheels, backflips, or pyramids to be seen—just seven beautiful young ladies performing a simple, though heartbreakingly inspiring routine, all to the continued silence from the crowd.

Then they followed up their routine with the vocal part of their performance by repeating a cheer along the lines of, "We're the Quakes, orange and white! Fight, fight, fight!" However, it was difficult to hear what they were saying because their relatively weak voices were swallowed up in the large arena.

By their final repetition, much of the crowd had come to their feet and had joined in to help them scream, "We're the Quakes, orange and white! Fight, fight, fight!" The standing ovation that followed put a thunderclap of an exclamation point to Vince Lombardi's quotation, "The measure of who we are is what we do with what we have!"

OC Quakes cheerleaders performing at ESPN Field House

* * *

I had the opportunity to become head coach of Trevor's Saddleback Valley Wolverine Challenger flag football team for their

2012 season. Once again, I was able to synergize what I'd learned through my recovery with what I knew about athletes with disabilities, leading to another case in point.

People who wind up in recovery are, almost without exception, disorganized and disorderly in almost every area of their lives. They'd have virtually no chance of getting sober without following the strict guidelines of a twelve-step program, attending meetings regularly, and taking direction from their sponsors.

Likewise, in their own unique way, people with disabilities tend to be disorganized and disorderly, to say the least. Consequently, taking what I learned from my sobriety, I tried to bring some much-needed organization to our practices and games.

We drew up some well-defined offensive plays, gave each player his or her own playbook, and worked on them at every practice.

On defense, we assigned players to specific positions so that they could learn their assignments during the repetition at practices.

Though official scores are not kept in Challenger flag football, by the end of our first season the Wolverines' unofficial record was 8-0-1, we "won" our Challenger Bowl game, and Trevor threw twenty-two touchdown passes.

We recruited some additional players from Trevor's basketball and floor hockey teams before the 2013 football season. The result was that our unofficial record was 9-0, we "won" our Challenger Bowl game again, and Trevor threw twenty-four touchdown passes.

We lost some veterans but gained some rookies prior to the start of the 2014 season. Nevertheless, our unofficial record ended at 8-0, we "won" our Challenger Bowl game again, and Trevor threw twenty-one touchdown passes.

Trevor and I "retired" from coaching and playing football in December 2015, but not before he threw twenty-two touchdown passes and led his team to an unofficial 9-0 record and a Challenger Bowl victory to cap off our final season.

2013 "Undefeated" Wolverines

Saddleback Valley Wolverines Pop Warner Challenger football team

* * *

Now—as I mentioned at the start of this chapter and against the backdrop of Trevor's athletic experiences and the Florida cheerleading competition—I want to explain what I meant when I said that tremendous spiritual blessings are available to everyone participating in extracurricular opportunities for people with disabilities.

I came to the conclusion some time ago that everyone who raises a disabled child, coaches a team of players with disabilities, teaches a special education class, starts a special-needs ministry at church, or even volunteers at a Special Olympics event has a chance to help make it an eternally significant experience for everyone involved. How?

Well, whether or not we consciously approach our involvement with the intent to share God's love, I believe God can use us "normal" advocates (at least that's how we wish to appear) as conduits through which He can shine the light of His love into the hearts, souls, minds, and bodies of those with perhaps more obvious disabilities.

Matthew 5:14, 16 declares, "You are the light of the world. . . . Let your light shine before men, that they may see your good deeds and praise your Father in heaven."

I believe that God is able to shine the light of His love through us and into the lives of the disabled whenever we give of our time and energy to help them enjoy richer and more meaningful lives. Of course, not every event necessarily needs to be an evangelistic crusade, but our unqualified acceptance and unconditional love for the disabled people in our lives will hopefully be used by God to reach and encourage them to make their own decision to accept and receive Jesus Christ as their Lord and Savior.

Furthermore, perhaps that light of God's love, when fully accepted by these special people and then reflected from their smiling countenances back onto the faces of the people whose lives they've touched—be it one stranger on a street or thousands of spectators at a cheerleading competition—might even plant the seed for a "normal" person's own decision of a lifetime, with that decision of a lifetime leading to an eternity of experiencing God's perfect love. And with that outcome, I guarantee you, the people that have crossed the paths of the special-needs children to whom we've ministered will always consider themselves, most richly blessed!

> But God chose the foolish things of the world to shame the wise; God chose the weak things of the world to shame the strong. He chose the lowly things of this world and the despised things—and the things that are not—to nullify the things that are, so that no one may boast before Him. It is because of Him that you are in Christ Jesus, who has become for us wisdom from God—that is, our righteousness, holiness and redemption. Therefore, as it is written: "Let him who boasts boast in the Lord."
>
> (1 Corinthians 1:27–31)

9

As Working for
the Lord

Toward the end of the summer of 2011, we heard from some friends at church about a job that had opened up with Major League Baseball's Los Angeles Angels of Anaheim.

The opening was for the position of greeter at their team store, where baseball hats, jerseys, and other Angels memorabilia are sold to fans attending the games. As near as I could tell, the only requirements for this job were an outgoing personality, a friendly disposition, a warm smile, and the ability to greet fans with "Welcome to the Angels team store!"

I thought Trevor might be perfect for this simple, though not easy, job.

Trevor and I drove up to Angel Stadium for the last home game of the season and were introduced to Eddie, the team store manager. He was a very nice guy and said to call him in a couple of weeks, which I did. He then asked me to send him an email as a reminder that Trevor was still interested in the job.

After that email and a few subsequent voice mails, I finally got ahold of him again. He said that the hiring decision was out of his hands and that I'd have to contact the HR department of the Anschutz Entertainment Group Merchandise division.

AEG is a multinational corporation that owns many stadiums and promotes concerts and athletic events around the world, as well as running the Angels team store concessions.

I was then able to connect with Jason, AEG's HR manager and also a very nice guy. He said, "Keep in touch. We haven't hired anyone yet. We'll let you know what we decide."

Over the course of several weeks, I kept asking various AEG personnel if they could at least give Trevor an interview. "If you don't think he can do the job," I said, "that's fine. We won't make a fuss, I promise. Just please give him a chance in an interview."

Jason said, "Okay, Mr. Hendershot. We're scheduling interviews for next week. Why don't you both come to Angel Stadium next Wednesday at ten o'clock? We'll interview Trevor then."

*　　*　　*

We got Trevor a new sport coat, a pair of nice slacks, and a cool tie with the Angels logo on it. We prayed and sang worship songs while driving up to the interview. After we were ushered into Store Manager Eddie's office, Trevor gave him a firm handshake, looked him in the eye, and said, "My name Trevor!"

We sat down in Eddie's office, and I handed Trevor's résumé to him, sparse though it was. He said, "Nice to see you again, Trevor," and began reading over the brief document.

Looking up, he said, "I see you like sports and have played on quite a few different teams."

"Yes, I play soccer, floor hockey, basketball, football," Trevor replied.

"Okay, that's good. Do you know anything about the Angels?" he asked.

"Yes, I do," Trevor answered and then proceeded to name many of the Angels players, both on the current team and those from their 2002 World Series championship season.

"That's very impressive!" Eddie said. "And what is this homecoming king deal about?"

I explained how Trevor was voted homecoming king by the Northwood High School student body. "Wow, I guess you're a pretty popular guy!" he exclaimed. "It looks like you've never actually had a job though, right?"

"Not yet," Trevor admitted.

Then Eddie looked further down Trevor's résumé and said, "I do see that you've had some retail training at Trader Joe's and Walgreens through your transition program. Can you tell me what your responsibilities were at those stores?"

Trevor responded, "I stock, face products, and do go-backs."

That's when Eddie leaned back in his chair and said, "You know, Trevor and Mr. Hendershot, this interview has now gone on for almost an hour, which is about forty-five or fifty minutes longer than I thought it might. Frankly, I can teach almost anyone how to stock, face products, and do go-backs. That would be simple enough."

I thought to myself, *Ok, that's that. Trevor did his best. We'll thank Eddie for his time and be on our way.*

But then Eddie went on, "However, I know from my years in the retail business that there are a few things I cannot teach—things like natural friendliness, a cheerful disposition and an engaging personality . . . all wrapped around a beautiful smile. And you, Trevor, have all of that and more! Our first home game is against the Kansas City Royals on Friday, April 6. Can you be there?"

"Yes, I can make that game," he said.

"Okay! In that case, I will be pleased to hire you for the position of Angels team store greeter."

Yay! But the interview wasn't quite over.

"There are just a few minor details we have to address before you're officially hired, Trevor," Eddie said. "First, we have to do a background check. Are you okay with that?"

"I'm good," Trevor said.

"We also have to administer a drug test. Is that okay?"

"What's that?" Trevor wondered.

"No big deal, Trevor," I quickly interjected. "There probably aren't any shots involved. You just pee into a cup they hand you."

"No way! I won't do that!" Trevor insisted.

Eddie was starting to show some concern, and so I implored Trevor, "Why not? Everybody who gets hired for a new job has to do a drug test!"

Trevor explained, "I'm not drinking my pee!" I guess he had assumed he would have to drink whatever was in the cup.

"No! You don't have to drink it! Just hand it back to the lab technician," I said.

Relieved, Trevor said, "Okay, I can do that."

The interview was over. We thanked Eddie and then sang worship songs and praised God all the way home.

*　*　*

Trevor started working in the Angels team store at their first home game in 2012, and he did a fantastic job—despite one minor hiccup that had to be worked out.

When the first Kansas City fans tried to come into the store wearing their Royals gear, Trevor told them, "Stop! Can't come in here! This store for Angels fans only!"

After it was explained to Trevor that anybody could come into the store, whether an Angels fan or not, he started telling opposing fans, "Okay, come in. Buy Angels hat!"

Trevor with Albert Pujols at Angel Stadium

On Trevor's birthday a few weeks later, the Angels surprised us with four great tickets, and our whole family was able to attend the game.

The president of the Angels, John Carpino, came into the store to wish Trevor a happy birthday and tell him, "You work your tail off around here!" He then presented him with a very generous birthday present: an autographed baseball from Albert Pujols, the Angels' future Hall of Fame player!

The chairman of the Angels, Dennis Kuhl, was scheduled to speak at a Chamber of Commerce event in Newport Beach (my hometown) a few weeks later, and we were invited to join him and talk about the occasion of Trevor's hiring by the Angels. Dennis told Trevor, "You're one of our best employees!"

Marcia Smith, a writer with the *Orange County Register* newspaper, interviewed us, and her story appeared on the front page of the paper's sports section.[1] The article talks about Trevor's Angels job, his love of sports, his homecoming king election, and his charming personality. It also tells of how our family's attendance at church and Bible studies has sustained us through the years. Finally, the article touches upon the fact that, at least for his father, Trevor's birth was an occasion for tears of great sadness; however, over the years (and too many times to count), Trevor's life has prompted his father to tears of great joy.

A long line of Angels fans were waiting to meet Trevor at the first game after the article appeared. Later in the season, the Angels had the *Register* article reprinted, framed, and mounted on the wall of the team store next to where Trevor stands at his post. Trevor has since become quite the local celebrity, and some fans are very disappointed if they attend a game and he happens to not be working that night. Trevor's boisterous, "Let's go, An-gels! Let's go, An-gels! Let's go, An-gels!" as well as his high fives, fist bumps, and joyful presence at every game he works lights up the lower level of the stadium for thousands of fans.

It is my firm belief that someday, if the Lord delays His return and then finally decides to send *His* angels to bring Trevor home to Him, Trevor will be able to repeat the words he's been practicing for so many years (but now perhaps in a quieter, though more glorious voice): "Let's go, An-gels!"

Then he'll immediately be escorted into heaven and the presence of his Lord and Savior Jesus Christ, where he'll hear the words every Christian longs to hear: "Well done, good and faithful servant!"

* * *

Later, during the summer of 2012, Trevor applied for the position of team store greeter with the National Hockey League's Anaheim Ducks. The Ducks team store manager, Sandy, really appreciated the joyful enthusiasm Trevor displayed during his interview, and so she hired him to be the Ducks team store greeter too!

Yay again!

Trevor with Ducks mascot Wild Wing

Unfortunately, the NHL went on strike and, as a result, lost half of their season. The Ducks' first home game was not until January 25, 2013. When Trevor finally was able to start working for the Ducks, the *Orange County Register* published another Marcia Smith article on Trevor in the sports section.[2]

Trevor's job with the Ducks is similar to his job with the Angels—except it requires him to yell, "Go, Ducks, go!" instead of, "Let's go, An-gels!" Other than that, both jobs require Trevor to joyfully stand for five hours or more and greet thousands of fans with high fives and/or fist bumps as they come into the stores.

* * *

Fox Sports West produced a five-minute video of Trevor working at Angel Stadium during the 2014 season. I was interviewed very briefly regarding the occasions of Trevor's birth and his hiring by the Angels, but the video mostly covers Trevor cheering for the Angels during their batting practice and his high-fiving of fans as they come into the store.

Albert and two other Angels players, Mike Trout (two-time All-Star Game and two-time American League MVP) and David Freese (2011 National League Championship Series and World Series MVP while playing for the Cardinals), are shown on the video describing Trevor's inspirational presence at the stadium.

The Angels team store manager, Martin Marin, talks about the excitement Trevor brings to the store as a valued employee. (This video can be accessed by using your smartphone to scan the QR code on the back cover of this book.)

* * *

I don't recall ever hearing of Trevor making the mistake of yelling for the wrong team or wearing the wrong uniform to either venue, but in my rush to get him to work on time, I've sometimes forgotten which way I'm supposed to turn on the Katella Avenue off-ramp on the 57 Freeway in Anaheim. Turning left takes us to Angel Stadium; turning right leads to Honda Center (one-half mile east) where the Ducks play. All I can do is continue to pray for the Lord's wisdom while muddling along as Trevor's chauffer and roadie.

At the end of every workday, whether working for the Angels or the Ducks, Trevor's palms are red from high-fiving, his knuckles are sore from fist-bumping, and his voice is hoarse from the thousands of fans he's greeted during the game—yet he's always more energized at the end of his shift than he was at the beginning.

If only each of us could similarly "find satisfaction in all his toil—this is the gift of God" (Ecclesiastes 3:13).

10

I Knew You Before You Were Born

Melissa and I have never ceased to be amazed by the wonderful things Trevor has thought, said, and done during his still relatively short life.

One of our initial prayers after Trevor's arrival was for the Lord's wisdom and discernment in raising him so that he would seek to follow God's will for his life and therefore be welcomed into heaven where our whole family would—by God's grace, mercy, and love—spend eternity together. For some time after his birth, however, we weren't sure whether Trevor would be able to articulate his faith in this lifetime, but on the other hand, we also weren't sure whether he might not end up leading one hundred people to Christ.

We did fervently pray that when we arrived in heaven, he might at long last be able to tell us in a clear, understandable, glorious voice, "Thank you, Mom and Dad, for being the kind of parents I needed you to be." Until that day comes, the many times we've heard, "I love you, Mommy," and "You my hero, Daddy," have comforted and encouraged us, especially in the aftermath of some of the numerous mistakes we've made during the course of raising all three of our sons.

Maybe you have just found out that your child has a disability. My advice to you is to "get into the boat" with the rest of us parents of children with special abilities because you'll be more blessed than you can possibly imagine.

The National Down Syndrome Congress and the National Down Syndrome Society are two great places to start meeting people involved in the wonderful world of Down syndrome. There are many other extraordinary organizations available for those challenged by autism, cerebral palsy, and other disabilities.

You might find additional encouragement by reading "Welcome to Holland," a short parable written by Emily Perl Kingsley in 1987.[3] Ms. Kingsley equates the discovery that your newborn child has a disability with the surprise that would occur if you departed on a vacation trip to Italy and instead your flight arrived in Holland.

You may have spent years anticipating a tour of the Roman Coliseum, seeing Michelangelo's *David*, and learning some simple Italian phrases to help in your visit, but when your plane touches down at the airport and the flight attendant says, "Welcome to Holland," it appears that all of your hopes and dreams have been dashed.

The important thing, Ms. Kingsley notes, is not that you've landed in an unpleasant place, but rather a *different* place. Your unplanned destination may seem less flashy, require learning a new language, and interacting with a whole new group of people, but Holland also has tulips, windmills, and Rembrandts.

Ms. Kingsley wisely concludes, "If you spend your life mourning the fact that you didn't get to Italy, you may never be free to enjoy the very special, the very lovely things . . . about Holland."

I believe that the tremendous blessings you'll experience by choosing to trust in God's plan for your special child will soon overshadow the initial sadness you may have felt when you first heard the words, "Welcome to Holland." I would go so far as to say that eventually you'll not only be able to say, "Welcome to Holland," to other new parents, but based on the blessings you've received from the life you've shared with your own special child, you'll be able to joyfully encourage new parents to embrace with all their hearts the reality of their unforeseen "move" to Holland.

And—a bolder assertion yet—you'll never, ever long for the life you once dreamed of, the ordinary life you would have known as the result of "living in Italy."

Now, don't get me wrong. I am not trying to discount the very real challenges—the additional time, financial burdens, and overall stress—involved in "moving to Holland." The tragic fact is that almost eighty percent of all marriages into which a disabled child is born end in divorce.

Of course, it's natural to experience worry, fear, and sorrow when we find ourselves facing unexpected trials.

The disciples had similar reactions when they found themselves with Jesus in a small boat on the storm-tossed Sea of Galilee. They cried out to Him, "Lord, save us! We're going to drown! Don't you care?"

Jesus didn't respond by saying, "This storm isn't that bad" or "This storm will be over soon." Instead, Jesus answered His disciples not by denying the reality of the situation but by demonstrating that He was the all-powerful God of the universe. He commanded the storm to, "Be still!" and the wind and waves immediately became calm.

By quieting down the storm, Jesus stirred up the disciples' hearts: "Who is this? Even the wind and the waves obey Him!" The Twelve realized that the Lord of the universe was with them in their boat.

Like the disciples, we who've been entrusted with a special child may also feel like we're drowning at times. But as the disciples learned, Jesus will always save us *through* storms, if not always *from* them. Our greatest weakness is usually our failure to rely on His strength. He never promised us smooth sailing in life, but we increasingly learn through our trials that He will always get into the boat with us and take us to the other side.

I pray that, like the disciples, you'll find your trust in God growing through, not diminishing in, the challenging times of life. What I do know for sure is that Trevor's arrival forever changed our family's relationship with God and eventually turned our focus toward the most important values of faith, family, and friends.

* * *

Educational mainstreaming, developed after the founding of Special Olympics, has been proved to benefit students with disabilities not only academically by facilitating higher scholastic achievements but also socially by increasing self-esteem and improving interpersonal skills.

As I've already indicated, we were extremely fortunate that when Trevor was born we already belonged to a wonderful church, Voyagers Bible Church in Irvine, California. Trevor's attendance there over the years proved to be a great blessing for the church, for our family, and for Trevor most of all.

This *spiritual* mainstreaming helped Trevor grow in his faith in God, encouraged him to worship his Savior with all of his heart, and in a safe church environment, exposed him to healthy interactions with people from many diverse and varied backgrounds. Trevor experienced spiritual mainstreaming at Voyagers during Sunday services as well as at the Influencers men's Bible studies on Friday mornings.[4]

Not only did he benefit but every member of these two groups had a chance to become acquainted with someone who had Down syndrome, possibly for the first time ever in many cases. One church elder told us, "Trevor was unquestionably a gift from God to our church." Our family felt comforted at church not only as we learned what Scripture had to say about those with disabilities but also by the supportive friendships we made there over the years. Trevor's loud, off-key singing during church services became a source of great joy to many parishioners during the twenty-four years we attended Voyagers.

After Taylor and Tanner left for college, Melissa and I felt the Lord calling us to attend a different church for the next season of our lives. While Trevor and I still continue to attend Influencers on Friday mornings at Voyagers, our family started attending Sunday church services at OC Harvest in Irvine. I think Trevor's worship style took some getting used to by the members of this new church family, but often after the service someone with reddened eyes would tell Trevor how much his singing inspired them.

After five years at OC Harvest, in July of 2017 we moved yet again to a newer, smaller church in Irvine, VISION City Church. Pastor Garid Beeler is a wonderful expository preacher, i.e., he preaches through the whole counsel of God, one verse/book at a time. The people are very friendly, there's great worship, and it's located less than five minutes from our house . . . so it's all good!

In light of Trevor's journey, I cannot recommend strongly enough to every parent to also spiritually mainstream your children by finding and attending a church where you *and* your child will feel welcomed. I'm not sure where our family, especially Trevor, would be without the biblical instruction and the spiritual growth we all experienced as a result of our church attendance over the last twenty-eight years.

Just as Trevor's educational mainstreaming during his school years in the Irvine Unified School District helped teach him academic and social skills, his spiritual mainstreaming at church helped him to develop not only a love for Jesus but also the composure he exhibits in the midst of very large crowds at Angel Stadium and the Honda Center. Both mainstreaming processes were instrumental in cultivating Trevor's outgoing personality, which in turn has led to the very, very *public* mainstreaming jobs he enjoys with the Angels and the Ducks.

Needless to say, of the three mainstreaming avenues, the greatest blessings came to Trevor from his spiritual mainstreaming because it helped him establish his close relationship with God, a relationship we'd all be wise to emulate. I believe that at least trying to walk with God the way Trevor walks with Him will put a smile on your face and a song in your heart too.

11

THE YEARS THE LOCUSTS
HAVE EATEN

Maybe you're not involved with anyone in the disabled community. Instead, perhaps you or someone you know is struggling with alcohol, drugs, or some other addiction.

I recommend grabbing onto the ladder of a twelve-step program that God has extended to you and countless others since Alcoholics Anonymous was founded in 1935.

Sadly, as I touched on earlier, some Christians hesitate to participate in twelve-step programs because they fear they'll be joining a cult. To be sure, some twelve-step groups do frown upon anyone naming Jesus as their Lord and Savior. Such groups may prefer that members use the term Higher Power in all references to God.

Nevertheless, "do not let your hearts be troubled" (John 14:27). I can reassure you that there are many biblically-based twelve-step groups where Christian testimonies are welcomed and encouraged.

Celebrate Recovery is a twelve-step program based on the Word of God, as opposed to secular psychological theories.[5]

And as I mentioned previously, Bill W. and Dr. Bob founded the program of Alcoholics Anonymous based on the tenets found in the Bible. In fact, the concepts of recovery, as well as the twelve steps, are fully supported by the principles found in Scripture.

* * *

One of my favorite passages in all of recovery literature is found on pages 216–217 in the third edition (1976) of *Alcoholics Anonymous* (a.k.a. the Big Book):

> When I came home, Clarence was sitting on the davenport with Bill W. I do not recollect the specific conversation that went on, but I believe I did challenge Bill to tell me something about A.A. and I do recall one other thing: I wanted to know what this was that worked so many wonders, and hanging over the mantel was a picture of Gethsemane and Bill pointed to it and said, "There it is," which didn't make much sense to me. There was also some conversation about Dr. Bob, and I must have said I would go down to Akron with Bill in the morning.[6]

Bill W. was referring to a painting of the scene in the garden of Gethsemane where Jesus went the night before He was to be crucified. It was at Gethsemane that Jesus cried out for God the Father to remove the necessity of His agonizing death on the cross. However, Jesus ultimately stated, "Yet not my will, but yours be done" (Luke 22:42).

The founder of Alcoholics Anonymous was referring to Jesus' substitutionary sacrifice for all who would believe in Him as the divine moment in time that "worked so many wonders."

Unfortunately, due to modern political correctness, this passage was deleted from the fourth edition (2001) of the Big Book. I can appreciate that the publishers did not want to offend anyone in this "progressive" era by including an undeniably Christian approach to recovery in the Big Book.

For sure, the world overall is a better and safer place for everyone when alcoholics of whatever religious, agnostic, or even atheistic stripe find themselves welcomed into a twelve-step program and are given the chance to become and remain sober.

Fortunately, page forty-five of the Big Book continues to state that the book's main objective is "to enable you to find a Power greater than yourself which will solve your problem." Over the years, many alcoholics with no religious background whatsoever have come to twelve-step meetings solely to quit drinking, found their initial Higher Power in the G.O.D. (Group of Drunks), and yet later came to believe Jesus' words: "I am the way and the truth and the life. No one comes to the Father except through me. If you really knew me, you would know my Father as well. From now on, you do know Him and have seen Him" (John 14:6-7).

Due to my recommitment to Jesus Christ as my Lord and Savior while in rehab and my participation in a twelve-step program, I have experienced much of what the Big Book promises on pages 83–84:

> If we are painstaking about this phase of our develop-ment, we will be amazed before we are half way through. We are going to know a new freedom and a new happiness. We will not regret the past nor wish to shut the door on it. We will comprehend the word serenity and we will know peace. No matter how far down the scale we have gone, we will see how our expe-rience can benefit others. That feeling of uselessness and self-pity will disappear. We will lose interest in selfish things and gain interest in our fellows. Self-seeking will slip away. Our whole attitude and outlook upon life will change. Fear of people and of economic insecurity will leave us. We will intuitively know how to handle situations which used to baffle us. We will suddenly realize that God is doing for us what we could not do for ourselves.[7]

Written by Bill W. in 1939, these promises have continued to resonate with people in recovery over the decades.

*   *   *

As I stated in chapter 3, the primary task of my initial sobriety was making direct amends to my family, friends, coworkers, and even strangers—at least those I could recall. But because my active alcoholic life was so characterized by memory losses from blackouts, there are no doubt more than a few people I'd harmed but whom I can't remember and therefore haven't been able to make amends to them.

After having been initially sober for about twelve years, and now in this second period of sobriety of twenty years, I reckon I've been sober for approximately thirty-two out of the last thirty-four years.

It seems safe to assume that anybody I may have harmed while I was drinking has probably either gone away or forgotten whatever personal injury I might have inflicted on them while I was drunk. I figure that I can walk anywhere in Newport Beach (where I grew up) or in Irvine (where I now live) with no fear of a person, place, or thing from my past. But then I went to Costco one day.

I was loading groceries into the trunk of my car when a woman pushing her cart behind me slowed down for a moment and gave me a funny kind of look. She kept going for a few seconds and then turned around and came back to my car.

She stopped and said something like, "You probably don't remember me, but I remember you. I recognize you. I know who you are."

Instantly my heart leapt into my throat. All my years of sobriety suddenly vanished, and I was immediately transported back to the years of mornings of pitiful and incomprehensible demoralization. I braced myself against the angry accusations that were sure to follow.

But then she asked, "You're Trevor's dad, aren't you?"

"That's me," I replied.

"I heard you speak some time ago about raising your son Trevor and your struggle with alcoholism."

I said, "Well, I've shared our story at a few different places, some more reputable than others."

She continued, "This was probably a few years ago now at our old church, Voyagers in Irvine. I think you spoke for about ten, fifteen minutes. Do you remember that morning?"

"I do remember that day."

"Well, what you shared really moved me that morning because I have a nephew with autism and an uncle who died of alcoholism. Your story had a great impact on me. I've always wanted to personally thank you for your testimony."

"Thank you for thanking me. You don't know what this means to me."

Then she gave me a hug and was gone.

*　*　*

I know I still have a long way to go in my journey of faith and sobriety, but I'm forever grateful to God for the extension of His grace, mercy, and love to me in the raising of our special son and for motivating me to grab onto the ladder of a twelve-step program so that I could remain sober all of these years. In the words of the psalmist:

> I waited patiently for the Lord;
> > He turned to me and heard my cry.
> He lifted me up out of the slimy pit,
> > out of the mud and mire;
> He set my feet on a rock
> > and gave me a firm place to stand.
> He put a new song in my mouth,
> > a hymn of praise to our God.
> Many will see and fear
> > and put their trust in the Lord.
> Blessed is the man
> > who makes the Lord his trust,
> who does not look to the proud,
> > to those who turn aside to false gods.
> Many, O Lord my God,
> > are the wonders you have done.

The things you planned for us
   no one can recount to You;
were I to speak and tell of them,
    they would be too many to declare.

(Psalm 40:1–5)

If God has carried me through all the challenges in my life in order to touch the life of that one woman on that one Sunday morning so many years ago, well, I've already been repaid for "the years the locusts have eaten" (Joel 2:25).

12

THE PAST WAS WRITTEN
TO TEACH US

In a sermon I heard some time ago, the pastor compared the efforts aviation investigators make to recover the so-called black boxes from aircraft that have crashed to the efforts of Christians who study Scripture and fellowship with other believers.

I'm not involved in the aviation industry, but I've done some additional research to learn more about black boxes. It became apparent to me that this analogy works not only for Christians but perhaps even more so for those people suffering through difficult life experiences such as addictions and disabilities. Let me share some of what I learned.

On every aircraft there are two indestructible, orange (painted so for ease of recovery), metal boxes:

- The flight data recorder (FDR) records electronic and mechanical data such as altitude, cabin pressure, air speed, and other specific parameters. When aviation experts recover this box and review the data, they can evaluate whether there was anything electronically or mechanically wrong with the aircraft that caused it to deviate from its flight plan and crash. If the experts determine there was a physical problem, then they have to further decide if this was a problem isolated to this one particular aircraft or perhaps a design flaw that may need to be corrected on all similar aircraft models.

- The cockpit voice recorder (CVR) records voice conversations in the cockpit, as well as any radio communication with other aircraft and air traffic controllers. After recovering this box, crash investigators gather fellow pilots and aviation engineers in a room and play back the recording to see if they can determine what was going on in the cockpit at the time of the crash. For instance, was the crew even aware of any difficulties? If so, what were they doing to try to correct the problem?

If the pilots' more personal conversations are recorded, then investigators will also bring in family and friends of the crew so they can hear their loved one's last words moments before the crash such as, "Sorry, John," or "I love you, Amy," or even, "God help us!" These voice recordings help investigators determine if pilot error caused or contributed to the crash. If pilot error was a factor based on what these cockpit conversations reveal, then training methods may need to be changed.

When people die tragically in aircraft disasters, determining the cause of the crash based on FDR and CVR information can mean that electronic and mechanical problems have to be corrected and/or improved in-flight operating procedures implemented so that similar accidents will not recur in the future. Accidents are frequently the result of both physical problems and pilot errors. Fortunately, we human beings have access to our own versions, so to speak, of both the flight data recorder and the cockpit voice recorder that can help us avoid "crashing" during our journey through life.

*   *   *

For Christians, the truths found in the Bible that tell us who we are, why we are here, and that our lives have eternal meanings are much like the data compiled in an FDR. When we study the Scriptures, we begin to appreciate the safety of following God's will (flight plan) for us. As we then walk by faith and in obedience to what the Bible clearly tells us to do, we can be confident that the Lord will lead us through our difficult circumstances, even when our future course is not so clear to us.

We also read in the Bible about the disastrous outcomes that occur when people choose to disobey and not follow God's will for their lives. The assimilation of Scripture into our heart, soul, and mind will help us truly understand that instead of trying to twist God's arm to get Him to conform His will to our wants and desires, we'd really be much better off just putting our entire lives into His hands.

Making obedience to Him our highest priority will not only help us to avoid "crashes" but also serve as the source of our greatest joy because we'll look at life from the perspective of eternity.

Paul wrote to the Romans, "Everything that was written in the past was written to teach us, so that through endurance and the encouragement of the Scriptures we might have hope" (Romans 15:4). Then we can truly learn from those who've gone before us and not have to experience every painful lesson in the crucible of our own suffering.

Just as the Bible provides spiritual FDR information, the fellowship we Christians enjoy with other believers corresponds to the CVR recordings that help pilots, engineers, and family members determine an aircraft crew's state of mind prior to their crash. Christians benefit greatly from being part of a congregation of believers who listen with compassionate understanding when they share one another's struggles and successes, where the daily challenges they face are heard, understood, and responded to with grace, mercy, and love.

This kind of Spirit-filled congregation provides its members with a safe environment where they can connect on a deep and meaningful level. The truth is that transparent fellowship with like-minded souls fulfills a need in us that cannot be met in any other way. Christians who exercise their uniquely God-given gifts, passions, and abilities help contribute to the instruction, edification, and remonstration of fellow believers in their community.

Paul told the Ephesians that in such a community, "the body of Christ may be built up until we all reach unity in the faith and in the knowledge of the Son of God and become mature, attaining to the whole measure of the fullness of Christ" (Ephesians 4:12-13).

Encouraging this type of communal growth, the author of the book of Hebrews exhorted believers to "not give up meeting together, as some are in the habit of doing, but let us encourage one another—and all the more as you see the Day approaching" (Hebrews 10:25).

* * *

In addition to relying on the FDR of Scripture and the CVR of fellowship, Christians are also called to make prayer such a vital part of our lives that we come to instinctively trust our all-knowing God with everything concerning our unknown future. Proactively making prayer our first response and not our last resort will help us to catch a glimpse of God's infinite perspective when facing any situation.

When we pray for God's wisdom, He helps us understand the FDR of Scripture, and when we pray with others, we strengthen our relationship with God as well as our relationships with those in our CVR fellowship.

Of course, the prayer of primary importance is the so-called sinner's prayer by which we ask to receive forgiveness for our sins and accept Jesus Christ as our Savior and Lord. (Please refer to chapter 2.)

We're also called to pray for guidance in all of our decisions as we walk with God over the course of our lives. Like a young child's parent who listens and tries to understand their toddler's feeble words, God hears and understands the softest cries of our lips as well as the deepest longings of our heart and brings them into line with His ultimate purposes for our lives.

Because His purposes for us will rarely, if ever, include a life free from suffering, we must pray for a faith that's grounded in our relationship with God and therefore won't be shaken or swept away when the winds of adversity strike.

Consider—and follow—Paul's instructions to the Romans to "be joyful in hope, patient in affliction, faithful in prayer"; his charge to the Colossians to "devote yourselves to prayer, being watchful and thankful"; and his call to the Thessalonians to "be joyful always; pray continually; give thanks in all circumstances, for this is God's will for you in Christ Jesus."

Knowing that God will either change our circumstances or use them to change us, I always pray that my family's thoughts, words, and actions would glorify Him and that our needs, wants, and desires would always be in harmony with His good, pleasing, and perfect will for our lives. Truly the most powerful position on earth is kneeling before the God of the universe.

* * *

My struggle with alcoholism taught me to look at my suffering not as a hindrance but as a pathway to spiritual growth that over the years has lead me closer to God through His Word and fellowship with His people. God knows that He wouldn't be able to accomplish everything He wants to in our lives if He didn't allow us to go through the experience of painful trials.

Before my alcoholic relapse in March of 1996, I had begun to rely on my own ability to deal with my problems. God showed me my weakness in order to teach me to rely on His strength.

I took pride in my successes and began to think I didn't need His help. He allowed me to fail so He could teach me that true success comes by His grace alone.

The result of His loving discipline was that I learned, to my great chagrin, that it's easier to look up to God in heaven when you find yourself flat on your back on earth.

While in rehab, I grabbed the ladder of a twelve-step program that the Lord can use to rescue those drowning in alcoholism. I learned that studying the Big Book of Alcoholics Anonymous was also like analyzing the data in a recovered FDR—on its pages, I was provided with insights regarding the reality of my alcoholism that have helped me to remain sober for many years.

I also learned that attending twelve-step meetings with others who share my addiction was like playing back the recordings in a CVR—listening to the voices of both the newly sober and those having many years of sobriety, as well as sharing my own experience, strength, and hope with them, has helped me to avoid many mistakes and maintain my sobriety one day at a time.

Likewise, regarding disabilities, availing ourselves of the numerous informational resources available on the internet, as well as participating in an appropriate special-needs support group, will help to alleviate many of the difficulties parents face when raising children with challenges.

*　*　*

Trevor once asked me, "Why you alcoholic?"

The best answer I could give him was, "I'm an alcoholic because I drank too much alcohol."

He told me, "Don't drink anymore!"—which is good advice for anyone of my bent.

While I know I have a predisposition to alcoholism, I also know I have to accept complete responsibility for all the sinful choices I've made and, unfortunately, will continue to make in my journey through life. It's easier to say, "I'm sick. I have a disease, and I can't help myself," than to say "I'm sorry. I was wrong, and I want to make things right."

Unless we acknowledge that our problems are rooted in the choices we've made, we'll never enjoy the complete healing that comes from being forgiven both by God and the people we have hurt. The apostle John put it this way: "If we confess our sins,

He is faithful and just and will forgive us our sins and purify us from all unrighteousness" (1 John 1:9).

As a Christian in recovery, I've also found it very helpful to meditate on the truths found in the original and long form of Reinhold Niebuhr's "Serenity Prayer." This version adds the following stanza to the shortened version found in chapter 2 of this book:

> Living one day at a time,
> Enjoying one moment at a time,
> Accepting hardship as a pathway to peace,
> Taking, as Jesus did,
> This sinful world as it is,
> Not as I would have it,
> Trusting that You will make all things right,
> If I surrender to Your will,
> So that I may be reasonably happy in this life,
> And supremely happy with You forever in the next.
> Amen.

13

Ask Where the Good Way Is and Walk in It

Maybe you're not struggling with either alcoholism or the challenges of a disability, but you are suffering due to some other difficult situation. Do you feel that your predicament is beyond repair? Have you given up hope for any solution? From his personal experience of God's faithfulness throughout the many triumphs and tragedies of his life, King David wrote in Psalm 34:18, "The Lord is close to the brokenhearted and saves those who are crushed in spirit."

David regarded the Lord's steadfast love and provision as positive proof that the omniscient, omnipotent, and omnipresent God of the universe knows us, cares about us, and is both willing and able to redeem any challenge in our lives to His eternal glory. David's expectation was not necessarily deliverance from each and every tribulation he faced but the sure hope of seeing God's goodness whatever the outcome of the trials he was enduring. He also wrote these words:

> I am still confident of this:
>> I will see the goodness of the Lord
>> in the land of the living.

> Wait for the LORD;
>> be strong and take heart
>> and wait for the LORD.

(Psalm 27:13–14)

Like David, we can expectantly wait for God to work out His perfect will for us. After all, our situations will never take Him by surprise, and He will always provide the solution, wisdom, hope, and guidance we need to persevere through our circumstances.

Whatever problems you're facing, consider applying what you've learned from the trials in your past to develop your own Synergy of Suffering in the midst of the trials you're dealing with today. Instead of fearing for the future when enormous obstacles appear in your path, send up a prayerful SOS to God, and He'll enable you to recall the lessons you learned from past sufferings and empower you to synergize those experiences into your walk of faith today and your trust in His plan for you tomorrow.

And then when we're also careful to read, meditate, and obey God's Word, when we seek out and listen to the wise counsel of concerned Christian friends, and when we prayerfully depend on the Holy Spirit's leading and moment-by-moment help, then no doubt we'll be able to say along with the prophet Samuel, "Thus far has the LORD helped us."

Samuel set up a stone monument to remind the Israelites of what God had done on their behalf in the past and to reassure them that He would continue to show His power to them in seemingly hopeless situations in their future. A backward glance at the monuments to God's former faithfulness in your own past can also give you the confidence to move forward by faith into your future.

*   *   *

God asked Jeremiah, "If you have raced with men on foot and they have worn you out, how can you compete with horses? If you stumble in safe country, how will you manage in the thickets by the Jordan?" God seems to be indicating to Jeremiah that He uses the earlier, easier challenges in our lives to prepare us for the later, harder ones to come.

Our family's initial Synergy of Suffering experiences occurred after we synergized what we learned by trusting God throughout the duration of our infertility with the lifetime of challenging years that we knew we would face after Trevor was diagnosed with Down syndrome soon after his birth.

As I've already described, Melissa took Trevor into her heart fairly quickly, but that wasn't so much my experience.

At first I wanted God to miraculously intervene, to supernaturally "fix" Trevor, and to give me the son I thought I deserved. Frankly, I'm not sure when I would have truly welcomed Trevor into our family if God hadn't helped me to recall what I had learned about His faithfulness during the five long years of infertility.

The slowly developing miracles I've experienced as Trevor's father were the divine interventions that I really needed. God used them to produce eternal blessings and greater spiritual maturity in my life.

* * *

Of course, since Trevor is the person with Down syndrome, the question must be asked, "Has he learned anything from his own Synergy of Suffering?" As it turns out, the negative actions inflicted on Trevor earlier in his life have helped him deal with some of the more unruly fans at Angel Stadium and Honda Center.

Trevor truly loves both of his jobs, and 99.9 percent of the fans who come into the stores are kind, gracious, and compassionate when they meet him. However, a few fans from other teams and/or those who've probably had too much to drink have cussed him out when he's said, "Let's go, An-gels!" or "Go, Ducks, go!" One even threw a beer cup at him when he told them, "No food or drink in store."

Trevor's job coach or another fellow employee is usually by

his side to prevent this sort of behavior, but if not, Trevor will debrief us about what happened on the way home.

When Trevor tells us that a drunk and obnoxious fan bothered him that shift—despite our prayers for his safety on the way up to the stadium—an embarrassing (to me) incident from Trevor's past unfortunately plays into the discussion. Trevor remembers that many years earlier there had been another drunk and obnoxious person in his life—me.

While I never cussed at Trevor or threw a beer cup at him, I'm well aware—and I tell Trevor this—that back then I desperately needed both Jesus as my Savior and sobriety in my life, so it's probably safe to assume that any out-of-control fans Trevor encounters today do too. That's why we always pray for the salvation and sobriety of the fans Trevor will come into contact with at both Angel Stadium and Honda Center.

The bottom line of Trevor's Synergy of Suffering, though, is that because God helped him overcome schoolyard bullies—and an alcoholic father—Trevor intuitively knows that God will help him overcome any drunk and disorderly fans who need Jesus and come through the team stores today. So rather than letting wild and crazy fans get him down, Trevor can instead make the choice to rejoice over the tremendous blessings he enjoys as a young man who has Down syndrome and yet is employed at two of the arguably coolest jobs in Southern California. Trevor remains cheerfully optimistic about tomorrow because he walks with Jesus today.

The decision to overcome *through* our suffering rather than to be overcome *by* our suffering is in front of us every day as well. If we make the daily choice to embrace an attitude of gratitude, then—like Trevor—our demeanor will not reflect the disappointment prompted by the circumstances around us but instead will reflect the joy that comes from the Lord living within us.

14

So That We Can Comfort Those in Any Trouble

When facing difficult circumstances, believers and nonbelievers alike may ask the most fundamental of human questions: Why is there so much pain and suffering in the world?

We know that God says in the book of Isaiah, "'My thoughts are not your thoughts, neither are your ways my ways,' declares the Lord. 'As the heavens are higher than the earth, so are my ways higher than your ways and my thoughts than your thoughts.'"

Nevertheless, any answers to questions regarding the prevalence of evil in the world would probably include the following:

First, God designed the universe. He established order on the earth; He designed wind, rain, and fire and their environmental effects; and He incorporated such natural laws as gravity and thermodynamics in the process. Of course, we need these natural phenomena in order to survive, and yet these same laws and principles can result in tragedy when foolishly ignored or managed incorrectly by us humans.

Second, this fallen, broken world where we live is the site of ecological disasters, catastrophic diseases, and untimely deaths—all of which are regrettable results of the sin that was brought into the world by the rebellion of man in the Garden of Eden.

Third, though God has prescribed definite limits to his evil behavior, Satan remains a cunning, powerful, and intelligent adversary who seeks to cause suffering in the lives of Christians through spiritual deception and physical harassment.

Fourth, because we are social beings and our lives are intertwined with the lives of other people, we do suffer when the sins of others negatively impact us.

Finally, our pain can be the result of our own sinful choices.

Whatever the cause of our suffering, if we're followers of Christ, I believe that our response should not necessarily be, "What would Jesus do?" but instead, "What would Jesus *have me* do?" After all, Jesus calmed the storm, gave sight to the blind, and raised the dead back to life. Because we obviously lack His divine nature, how should we humans—we who are "jars of clay"—respond to suffering?

The apostle Paul wrote these words in 2 Corinthians 1:3–7:

> Praise be to the God and Father of our Lord Jesus Christ, the Father of compassion and the God of all comfort, who comforts us in all our troubles, so that we can comfort those in any trouble with the comfort we ourselves have received from God. For just as the sufferings of Christ flow over into our lives, so also through Christ our comfort overflows. If we are distressed, it is for your comfort and salvation; if we are comforted, it is for your comfort, which produces in you patient endurance of the same sufferings we suffer. And our hope for you is firm, because we know that just as you share in our sufferings, so also you share in our comfort.

Again, God apparently hasn't comforted us just to make us comfortable but to strengthen us so that we can comfort others. So how do we comfort others in their difficulties? If we've allowed God to use the sufferings in our own life to accomplish everything that He desires to do in and through us, then we can pass on His hope and encouragement to others who are also similarly suffering. This ability to comfort others does not necessarily come from having a dynamic personality, eloquent articulation, or even vast biblical knowledge. Rather, it's the quiet listener with a hand to hold, the compassionate friend with a heartfelt hug, and the sympathetic fellow sufferer with tears to share who provide the most meaningful comfort to those who are struggling during times of trouble.

* * *

We must prayerfully hope that the way we respond to our challenges will bear witness to our spouses, families, neighbors, coworkers, and even strangers on the street of the faith, hope, and love we have in Jesus. Our thoughts, words, and actions should testify to everyone we meet of our belief that:

- God is in control of every tribulation.
- He has a divine, though often unexplained, reason for our sufferings.
- He will supply us with the strength to stand firm in the face of any difficulty.
- We are to submit to whatever He wants to teach us through our trials.

The end result of a life transformed by trials will be an enduring blessing both in this present, temporal life and the future, eternal life to come.

* * *

The bottom line of Trevor's and my story is this: The Christian life should be a window through which others see Jesus. Has my life revealed to others that I know Him? Not often enough. Can other people see that my heart has been transformed? Well, maybe sometimes. I've always tried to be the Christian man, husband, father, son, brother, and friend who would be pleasing to God, but in light of all the willful sins, foolish mistakes, and embarrassing pratfalls I've taken over the years, I doubt that my testimony has brought any meaningful degree of hope or encouragement to any more than a handful of the people that I know.

Trevor's life, however, has been an undeniably positive testimony of the joy to be found in living for the Lord with all your heart, soul, mind, and body. Trevor's optimistic personality, cheerful demeanor, and impassioned cheering at his jobs distinguish him as one of Christ's greatest ambassadors.

Fellow employees have remarked that Trevor's presence never fails to brighten up their day and that his admirable work ethic encourages them to apply themselves more fully to their jobs. Trevor gives hope to parents and their disabled children who come to Angel Stadium and Honda Center just to meet him and be inspired to reach for their own dreams.

I feel Trevor's most important mission, however, is his edification of fellow believers at church through his unbridled friendliness and uninhibited singing during Sunday morning services and Friday morning men's Influencers gatherings. Parishioners have told us over the years that they wish they could worship with their hearts like Trevor does. They've stated that he's the most Spirit-filled person they've ever met and that they're always so glad to see him at church, not only because his presence lights up the sanctuary but also because then they know for sure that they haven't missed the rapture!

* * *

Trevor recently asked Melissa a very revealing question: "Did God give me Down syndrome?"

She replied, "Yes. Are you okay with that?"

His response spoke volumes: "Yeah, I'm good."

I know that Jesus said, "There is only One who is good." Nevertheless, Trevor's answer prompted me to review the first twenty-six years of our life together. The inescapable conclusion I came to was that Trevor's birth was neither the happiest nor the saddest moment of my life but rather one of the *greatest* moments of my life. For that was the day Melissa and I received nothing less than a very special gift from the Lord on high: a boy whom He had known about since before the beginning of time, a son whom He had brought into the world exactly the way He wanted him to be.

Of course, those statements are true for all of our children. There's not an extra hair on their heads, let alone extra chromosome in their bodies. They have all been created in God's image (Genesis 1:27), and He's given them to us as a great and awesome responsibility and *privilege*, to train up and take care of for Him and on His behalf for as long as we remain on earth.

Finally, while I still would not wish an unredeemed disability or untreated alcoholism on anyone, with all the prayers, support, and love we've received from our friends, relatives, and church fellowships over the first twenty-six years of Trevor's life—not to mention all the prayers, support, and love that I've personally received over the last twenty years of my sobriety—I am able to declare today that Melissa and I just love our special son, Trevor William Hendershot, with all of our hearts, and with the whole earth as our witness, we would not have traded him or what God has taught us about His grace, mercy, and love through his life or through my struggle with alcoholism for anything or with anyone in the world.

And then lastly, but absolutely, positively not least, while I still would not consider myself to have been the best choice to raise a son with Down syndrome, nor even that good of an example of someone in recovery, I am able to declare today that by the grace of God, with the love of our Lord and Savior Jesus Christ, and through the power of the Holy Spirit, we—Bob's son with Down syndrome and Trevor's dad, recovering alcoholic—do consider ourselves, most richly blessed!

May the name of the Lord be praised!

EPILOGUE

A visiting pastor declared at an Influencers men's retreat in early May of 2014, "Consider what breaks your heart, because that's where God is calling you into ministry."

Since receiving Jesus Christ as my Lord and Savior in 1987, I've taught our sons' Sunday school classes with Melissa, spoken at college fraternities regarding drug and alcohol issues, led several men's Bible studies, fed homeless people on Skid Row, and sung Christmas carols to elderly nursing-home residents.

While my participation in these ministries was definitely rewarding and the ministries' recipients themselves seemed to have been blessed, at least to some degree, my decision to engage in them was never compelled from the emotions of a broken heart.

Consequently, the pastor's exhortation caused me to think about what does break my heart.

*   *   *

In late 1989, when Melissa was sixteen weeks pregnant with Trevor, the then-standard alpha-fetoprotein (AFP) test was administered to diagnose whether our child might be encumbered with challenges such as Down syndrome. Miraculously, the test results indicated an absence of any so-called "abnormalities," and therefore we only discovered God's big surprise for us after Trevor came into this world.

In retrospect, we were very fortunate to not have been faced with making a decision that could have led to us missing out on one of the greatest blessings in our lives. The now-standard pregnancy-associated plasma protein-A (PAPP-A) test can diagnose Down syndrome after only nine weeks of pregnancy. As a result, potential mothers regretfully now have so little time to bond with their babies growing inside them that ninety percent of those so diagnosed become victims of abortion.

This is what breaks my heart.

* * *

Albert Pujols was so taken by Trevor's joyful enthusiasm for his job in the Angels team store that his Pujols Family Foundation drafted a proposal to "Trevorize" every Major League Baseball stadium in America. In other words, they launched a campaign to encourage MLB teams across the country to hire individuals with Down syndrome to work in jobs similar to the one Trevor enjoys with the Angels. Yay!

Their twelve-page proposal began by introducing Trevor as "one of the rising stars in the Los Angeles Angels' organization" with an "unmistakably kind, genuine, and engaging spirit" who was hired because he was "the right person for the job." The proposal continued by suggesting specific and general guidelines to ensure the successful implementation of the "Trevorization" employment process throughout Major League Baseball. The Pujols Family Foundation graciously asked for our help in composing the following suggested employee qualification requirements:

- Loves meeting people, has an enthusiastic personality, and is a cheerful team player.
- Enjoys excitement of raucous crowds and chaotic atmosphere of baseball stadiums.
- Follows directions, appreciates positive praise, and accepts constructive criticism.
- Maintains friendly demeanor when encountering unruly fans of visiting teams.

- Remains physically energetic and mentally alert for duration of work shift.

In summary, the proposal described how the tremendous long-term social and financial benefits that would accrue to Major League Baseball as the result of "Trevorizing" their stadiums would far outweigh any potential short-term challenges involved in hiring someone with a developmental disability. MLB Commissioner Bud Selig, in fact, approved and signed off on the proposal in 2014. However, after twenty-two years in office, Commissioner Selig decided to retire, and so final approval will have to wait for new Commissioner Rob Manfred to sign off on the proposal.

* * *

In December 2013 during the L.A. Kings at Anaheim Ducks hockey game, some Kings fans verbally harassed Trevor while he was working as team store greeter. Nothing too unusual about that—encounters with disorderly fans are pretty much part of Trevor's job description. What *was* unusual occurred when another Kings fan decided to make amends for Trevor's mistreatment and took up a collection to buy a Ryan Getzlaf (the Ducks' team captain) jersey for Trevor.

Several other Kings fans made generous contributions to the cause, and the jersey was presented to Trevor at a game later in the season. Trevor has often been blessed with cards and presents from hometown Angels and Ducks fans, but to receive such a wonderful gift from the fans of an opposing team was really quite remarkable, especially considering the intense rivalry that exists between these two teams and their fans.

As a result of Trevor's impact on these Kings fans, the thought came to mind that perhaps an attempt should be made to Trevorize the National Hockey League just like Major League Baseball. Trevor's ability to soften the hearts of the fans of his team's greatest rival suggests that other employees with Down syndrome could make identical impacts on the fans attending games of their local NHL teams. Seven out of the thirty total NHL teams are located in Canada, and so if this particular proposal goes through, it could lead to the Trevorization of much of North America. Staples Center in downtown Los Angeles appears to be the logical place to start for a number of reasons.

As indicated in chapter 9, Trevor was hired by the Anschutz Entertainment Group Merchandise division for the team store greeter job at Angel Stadium. AEG also owns the L.A. Kings, winners of the Stanley Cup in 2012 and 2014, and Staples Center, which is the Kings' home arena, located thirty miles north of Anaheim's Angel Stadium and Honda Center. Fortunately, the same AEG personnel that hired Trevor and continue to oversee his employment at Angel Stadium are likewise involved in the corresponding operations at Staples Center. We're hoping that Trevor's successful employment with the Angels will encourage AEG to Trevorize Staples Center too.

Additionally, another "coincidence" I believe is comparable to Albert's signing with the Angels on December 8, 2011, occurred when Darryl Sutter took over as head coach of the Kings nine days later on December 17, 2011. Coach Sutter's son, Chris, has Down syndrome, as does Albert's daughter, Isabella. Though we haven't met the Sutters yet, I learned some things about Darryl from the interviews he's done for newspapers and on television.

For one, I know we both appreciate the tremendous blessings that our sons have brought into our lives and those of our families. In addition, Darryl understands that people with Down syndrome yearn for lives of meaning and purpose proportional to what "typical" people might enjoy. He also realizes that part of our jobs as parents of children with Down syndrome includes doing whatever we can to help them succeed in their desired vocations.

We hope then that Darryl might feel called on some level to help individuals with Down syndrome maximize their potential as employees through the Trevorization of the National Hockey League. The extended Sutter family is uniquely positioned to assist in this endeavor since Darryl is one of six brothers who played, coached, and/or became general managers on thirteen of the NHL's thirty teams.

The Sutters' involvement as one of hockey's most famous families would definitely open doors for the Trevorizing of National Hockey League arenas, just like Albert Pujols could be instrumental in facilitating the Trevorization of Major League Baseball stadiums.

Finally, Staples Center is the only arena in the world that is home to four professional sports franchises—in addition to the Kings, the NBA's Lakers and Clippers and the WNBA's Sparks also play their home games there. Possibly down the road, individuals with Down syndrome could be hired to commence the Trevorization process in professional basketball.

* * *

I personally think that if God's will *is* to Trevorize MLB stadiums, NHL arenas, and other venues, then eternal purposes are attainable far beyond just providing amazing occupations for individuals with Down syndrome—as noble an enterprise as that may be.

To illustrate: We met a couple pregnant with a Down syndrome baby and still undecided on whether or not to terminate the life of their child. However, meeting Trevor and seeing the blessings he brought to those around him strengthened their decision to bring their baby into this world. Is it possible that God's highest intention for the Trevorizing of stadiums might be to provide living, breathing, pro-life testimonies for couples living in New York, Boston, Calgary, and other cities throughout the United States and Canada?

Conceivably, if someone finds out they're pregnant with a Down syndrome child, then a concerned friend, family member, or church parishioner would be able to encourage them to high-five Tommy at Yankee Stadium or say hello to Jasmine at Fenway Park or fist-bump Chris at the Saddledome, or to plead with them to find and visit the closest sports venue that is currently being Trevorized. Hopefully they'll also be inspired to make the eternally correct decision to bring their child into the world—a decision I guarantee they would never regret.

Our hope is that through the Trevorization of stadiums and arenas across North America, not only will this frequently over-looked population have access to more exciting employment op-portunities but also one more life of a child with Down syndrome could be saved and one more set of parents-to-be could be blessed beyond measure. And that makes my heart feel better already.

* * *

What about those less-developed locations in the world that lack the latest medical technologies such as prenatal testing? Places where there's never been an advance warning of a special-needs child before birth or any support groups, athletic programs, or mainstreaming after his or her arrival? Have the destinies of the babies born with Down syndrome in these countries improved from the tragic fates I referred to in chapter 4? Sadly, the answer is usually no.

According to statistics, babies with Down syndrome are con-ceived approximately once out of every eight hundred to one thousand pregnancies, and yet missionaries report that individ-uals with Down syndrome are nowhere to be found in many for-eign lands. Towns and villages of any sizable population should statistically have at least one representative, so where might these missing individuals be?

Tragically, if the past is prologue, the males may have been sold into lives of backbreaking slave labor—sunrise to sun-down, seven days a week. Females may have been condemned to lives of abuse-filled prostitution—with a cot and a window-less room as their "home." "Suicide" bombers may have only been unsuspecting individuals with Down syndrome who were asked to carry a bomb-filled backpack and wander out into a crowded marketplace. The explosives were then detonated by remote control.

That is what *really* breaks my heart.

Is there any way to influence cultures around the world with the pro-life message that the lives of people who have Down syndrome are incredibly precious, infinitely valuable, and eternally significant? Would Trevorizing stadiums internationally help to accomplish that goal?

The AEG Facilities division owns and operates more than one hundred sports and entertainment venues located inside and outside the United States. A partial listing would encompass:

- Forty arenas, including locations in Belgium, Turkey, Germany, China, and Scotland.
- Forty clubs and theaters, including locations in England and Australia.
- Twelve stadiums, including locations in Russia, Sweden, and Brazil.
- Ten convention centers, including locations in Malaysia and Oman.

AEG's owner, Philip Anschutz (Sigma Chi fraternity, University of Kansas, 1961), has been "dedicated to using our resources to enrich the lives of children and families in need" since founding his company in 1999. Anschutz Entertainment Group has achieved well-deserved financial success in their various business operations, but their commitment to "doing our part in the communities in which we do business as well as in our world" will be their most significant legacy.[8]

What better avenue could there be for AEG to fulfill their stated mission to "give the world reason to cheer" than to Trevorize their international venues with employees who have Down syndrome? Imagine the difference God could make in the lives of individuals, families, and communities wherever employees with Down syndrome, like Trevor, were allowed to survive, thrive, and bless the lives of those around them through their employment at AEG facilities.

* * *

Our family will always be grateful to both AEG and the Angels for looking beyond Trevor's disability when they initially hired him to be their team store greeter. Trevor, for his part, claimed this life-changing employment opportunity as his pulpit from which to preach the message that every human being, whether disabled or not, is created in the image of God and therefore valuable beyond measure.

Since the start of the 2012 season, Trevor's Angel Stadium "sermons" have struck chords with so many fans, fellow employees, and the Angels players themselves, inspiring Albert's Pujols Family Foundation to promote the Trevorizing of every MLB stadium.

We will also always be grateful to the Anaheim Ducks for hiring Trevor as their team store greeter, which has led to the Trevorizing of Honda Center since the 2013 season. Again, we hope that Coach Sutter, perhaps in conjunction with Commissioner Gary Bettman, might be encouraged to help with the Trevorization of every NHL arena.

AEG's worldwide company newsletter published an article about Trevor soon after he was hired to work at Angel Stadium back in 2012. Our vision is that God might use the developing Trevorization of MLB stadiums and NHL arenas to inspire AEG's corporate personnel to sow the seeds of Trevorizing even further by hiring employees with Down syndrome to work at their venues wherever they may be located around the world.

We are in the process of forming a 501(c)(3) nonprofit corporation, Angels for Higher, to help facilitate the gainful employment of individuals with Down syndrome at sports stadiums across the United States, North America and around the world.

> No eye has seen,
>   no ear has heard,
> no mind has conceived
>   what God has prepared for those who love Him.

(1 Corinthians 2:9)

AFTERWORD

"Do all the good you can, by all the means you can, in all the ways you can, in all the places you can, at all the times you can, to all the people you can, as long as ever you can." Heavenly Father, You have made each of us unique and special, so please show us how You want us to use the special talents You have given us to glorify You.

—Billy Graham

God seems to prefer availability rather than innate ability when calling on Christians to carry out His good works. Apparently, the Lord chooses ordinary people to do extraordinary things so that their achievements can only be ascribed to His divine intervention.

It also appears that God even uses unordinary people, like those with Down syndrome, to accomplish great things to His glory. Service in His kingdom then is not just reserved for those Christians who have it all going on physically, mentally, and emotionally.

On the contrary, when those with perhaps more discernable challenges are motivated by their difficulties to pursue deeper and more meaningful relationships with God, then their sufferings will actually have been a help rather than a hindrance in their quest to be of service to Him. When those with disabilities grow closer to God, they'll learn more of His grace, mercy, and love, with the end result being that any questions of "Why me, God?" will inevitably transform into "What are Your plans for me, God?"

> For the eyes of the Lord range throughout the earth to strengthen those whose hearts are fully committed to Him.
>
> (2 Chronicles 16:9)

*   *   *

Fruitful service to God is contingent upon the alignment of our heart's desires with His divine will. Thankfully, our family is "all in" regarding any attempts to implement the Trevorization of venues in the United States, across North America, and around the world. We must always remember to write our plans in pencil and give God the eraser, but the following compendium summarizes where each of us currently feels called to serve.

ROBERT

We're hoping to have the opportunity to make presentations at MLB stadiums and NHL arenas regarding the benefits and challenges of hiring individuals with Down syndrome to work in their team stores, and to Down syndrome associations explaining the opportunities available at their local sports venues. Trevor and I would also be honored to share our testimony at churches regarding our journey through life together.

MELISSA

Melissa has experienced many changes in curriculum during her thirty years as a kindergarten teacher—from wooden blocks to iPad research, from finger painting to computer graphics, and from playing house to preparing for careers. And yet as an ambassador of Christ, her career mission remains the same: to instruct, encourage, and nurture her young students; to occasion-ally minister to their inexperienced parents; and to faithfully interact with her fellow teachers and school administrators.

Melissa also has a book to write, *Through Trevor's Eyes*, which we trust will enable children (and their parents) to vicariously experience and then personally embrace Trevor's beautifully simple and simply beautiful view of the world.

TAYLOR

Taylor graduated cum laude in 2014 with a BA degree in art from Westmont College, a private Christian college located just south of Santa Barbara, California. Taylor's compassionate heart is leading him into the teaching profession, just like Melissa. He's also a talented artist who helped design and develop the graphics for this book.

Taylor's future plans include composing a graphic-novel-style adaptation of Trevor's story, which could then be translated into foreign languages and distributed among the majority of cultures in the world without access to large sports stadiums yet are still in need of exposure to the special needs, pro-life message found in Trevorizing.

TANNER

Tanner graduated summa cum laude from Westmont College in 2016 with a BA degree in political science. He's considering a career as an attorney with a possible focus on international relations, while currently working as the development coordi-nator for the Jodi House Brain Injury Support Center.

A gifted speaker, Tanner could be called upon to further the cause of Trevorizing in a manner similar to how Solomon was charged by his father, David, to finish the good works that the king had planned but wasn't able to actualize.

Trevor

Trevor could have questioned his ability to serve God as the result of having Down syndrome and a dysfunctionally alcoholic father, but his heavenly Father looked past these challenging circumstances to the impact he would make in his world. He could have complained about the unfairness of life, but since his suffering encourages him to spend most of his waking hours in prayer, worship, and fellowship with other believers, his life joyfully proclaims God's goodness to everyone he meets.

He may have asked, "Why me?" and yet as God's implicit answers continue to unfold throughout the course of his life, Trevor's testimony continues to resonate in a language loud enough for the whole world to hear.

* * *

> Lord, help me to do great things as though they were little, since I do them with Your power; and little things as though they were great, since I do them in Your name.
>
> —Blaise Pascal,
> 17th-century French inventor,
> mathematician, and philosopher

Great Things

I conjectured during the testimony I shared at our church on the first Father's Day after Trevor's birth that he might eventually lead one hundred people to Christ. Trevor may not have verbally led anyone to Christ over the last twenty-six years, but he's been more than faithful with the one talent gifted to him by God and articulated by St. Francis: "Wherever you go, preach the gospel. If necessary, use words."

As the result of Trevor's faithfulness throughout earlier circumstances at men's retreats, Northwood High School, Angel Stadium, and Honda Center, hopefully God will indeed give the green light to the future blessings that would ensue from the Trevorization of stadiums across the United States, North America, and ultimately around the globe.

God's unlimited power has so multiplied the limited ability of this unordinary individual that not only have tens of thousands of baseball and hockey fans already been blessed in Southern California but perhaps eventually, by extension, hundreds of thousands of baseball and hockey fans across North America will be as well. Then ultimately, perhaps by further extension, millions of sports fans will be blessed through the Trevorizing of the world.

> "Now to Him who is able to do immeasurably more than all we ask or imagine, according to His power that is at work within us, to Him be glory in the church and in Christ Jesus throughout all generations, for ever and ever! Amen.

> (Ephesians 3:20)

LITTLE THINGS

We know that one of life's greatest certainties is its uncertainty, but if we've submitted our plans to God, we can still enjoy His peace even when unanticipated developments require changes in direction.

Since we've absolutely no control over how the men and organizations we hope become involved in Trevorizing decide to spend their valuable time, energy and resources, it's definitely within the realm of possibility that Trevor's influence may not extend beyond Angel Stadium and Honda Center.

We just pray that we'll be able to display His peace even if, for whatever reason, Trevorization never develops into a national or international phenomenon.

Of course this type of a response is easier to write down in a book than it is to live out in life on earth. All we can do is continue to pray for God's will to be done, whether or not that would include His intervention according to *our* will.

Jesus often preached to large gatherings, and yet he was more concerned with the few who came with "ears to hear" than with the total number of people in the crowd. Jesus cared more about the salvation of individuals like Zacchaeus, the invalid at Bethesda, and the Samaritan woman at the well than about His popularity among the masses. He was never inconvenienced when called to minister to anyone who needed His healing touch, because He never underestimated the value of one human soul.

Trevor's most important "appointments" have also tended to be one-on-one interactions—chiefly with fans as they come through the team stores' doors. Hundreds of fans continue to seek out Trevor's high fives, fist bumps, and words of encouragement that he dispenses via his one-at-a-time, one-of-a kind ministry. Our whole family prays we never forget that serving God in the little things is not a stepping-stone to greatness—it is greatness.

Who despises the day of small things?

(Zechariah 4:10)

Taylor, Robert, Tanner, Trevor and Melissa

POSTSCRIPT

The overall theme of *Angel for Higher* describes the process through which God answered my SOS prayers for help during my struggles with alcoholism and the challenges of Trevor having Down syndrome. God did this by synergizing the practical lessons He taught me in my recovery with the spiritual lessons He taught me as Trevor's dad.

In other words, what I learned in my sobriety has helped me to be a better father to Trevor, and what I received from Trevor has helped me to remain sober for over twenty years. My life has therefore been blessed with spiritual, emotional, and physical salvation, while Trevor's life has been enriched almost beyond measure from the result of our following God's Synergy of Suffering will for our lives.

*   *   *

When I think of the many things I've learned in my sobriety that helped me to be a better father to Trevor, I believe dancing for him on the sidewalk probably had the most lasting influence in his life. As indicated in chapter 3, his clapping and my dancing were part and parcel of the living amends I needed to make to Trevor for the harm I'd done to him while drinking. My dancing demonstrated to Trevor in a language he could understand that I was still sober, loved him with all of my heart, and would not have traded him for anything or anyone in the world.

The healthy development of Trevor's self-esteem was the greatest blessing that ensued from our Three Stooges performances.

Trevor realized while still very young that because he had Down syndrome, he needed a special bus to take him to a special school. He also came to realize that his daddy, out of love, would dance for him every morning before he took that bus to the school. Trevor eventually came to realize something of infinitely greater importance: that he needed a Savior to die for his sins and that Jesus—out of love—chose to die for all of our sins on the cross.

By accepting God's divine plan for our salvation—a synergy of His mercy (not getting what we deserve) with His grace (getting what we don't deserve)—our "highs" are kept from pridefully soaring too high, and our "lows" are kept from despairingly sinking too low.

* * *

> Remain in me, and I will remain in you. No branch can bear fruit by itself; it must remain in the vine. Neither can you bear fruit unless you remain in me. I am the vine; you are the branches. If a man remains in me and I in him, he will bear much fruit; apart from me you can do nothing. If anyone does not remain in me, he is like a branch that is thrown way and withers; such branches are picked up, thrown into the fire and burned. If you remain in me and my words remain in you, ask whatever you wish, and it will be given you. This is to my Father's glory, that you bear much fruit, showing yourselves to be my disciples.

> (John 15:4–8)

I doubt many people outside of our immediate family would have ever heard of Trevor if not for his abiding relationship with Jesus Christ. Trevor's intimacy with God produces spiritual fruit in every place and with everyone in his life. Trevor continues to remain in close fellowship with Jesus through his adherence to his own three-part unspoken aphorism:

Think Eternally . . . Serve Faithfully . . . Live Joyfully

THINK ETERNALLY

Trevor's focus is not on the things of this world but rather on that which has eternal value—faith, family, and friends.

Faith. Trevor carries a dog-eared copy of "God's Promises" everywhere he goes and can summon up the Bible verses inside quite effectively if necessary to make a point. I once reprimanded him after church for clapping and singing too loudly during worship, and so he read to me Psalm 47:1–2: "Clap your hands, all you nations; shout to God with cries of joy. How awesome is the Lord Most High, the great King over all the earth!" Should I have disagreed with the commands of Scripture?

He's often overcome with emotion while reading Bible passages or worshipping. When riding in our car, he'll sometimes cry out, "Jesus in the clouds!"

Melissa or I will then ask him, "What's He doing?"

Trevor will reply with something like, "He's standing there with His arms open."

Though we're never quite sure of what to make of his visions, I must confess that we're always very relieved when it turns out not to have been his Stephen moment (Acts 7:55–56).

Family. He absolutely loves his "brudders," his "beautiful mommy," and "my hero daddy." One time I was solemnly driving our car after a business deal I'd been working on failed to come through—again. Our sons were sitting in the back, Melissa was in the passenger seat, and I was muttering to God—again. A worship song came on the radio, and Trevor started singing along—well, sort of. His off-key voice wove in and out of the song's melody.

Then Tanner's distinctive baritone joined in, and Taylor's wonderful tenor soon followed. All three voices harmonized into one of the most beautiful a cappella concerts I'd ever heard: "It's all about you . . . all about you, Jesus." Melissa and I had tears in our eyes as we listened to this gentle reminder of what's really important.

Friends. Trevor instigates friendliness with everyone he meets. He's made dozens of friends over the course of his life using the simple tools that we all have at our disposal: a cheerful smile, high fives, fist bumps, encouraging words, and the occasional hug—if and when indicated.

Trevor's ultimately very discerning in regards to where somebody is truly coming from, but he always gives strangers the benefit of the doubt at first so he makes friends with them quite easily. His personality disarms even the most unlikely potential companions.

I remember taking Trevor to an Angels game when he was about ten years old. We sat next to a couple of empty seats, and since nobody had arrived by the third inning, I assumed they'd remain vacant for the rest of the game. Then I noticed two motorcycle gang member–types heading up the aisle next to where Trevor was sitting. Great, just perfect!

I asked Trevor if he wanted to switch places, but he said, "No, I'm good." I figured we were really in trouble after the two gentlemen plopped down—loud, obnoxious, and reeking of beer. The guy sitting next to Trevor had a very lifelike tattoo of a snake emblazoned on the calf of his left leg.

Of course, Trevor had to poke the tattoo with his index finger and declare, "Cool snake."

The guy glared at Trevor, then at me, and then back at Trevor and gruffly asked, "Well, whataya think of this one?" and he rolled up his left sleeve to reveal the tattoo of an arguably attractive female space alien.

Trevor perused her visage for a moment and then exclaimed, "Ooh la la!"

The bikers busted out laughing and then spent the rest of the game chatting with Trevor about the Angels, tattoos, and life in general.

When it came time for us to leave, I told the bikers what I always try to remember to say after serendipitous encounters of this sort: "Thank you for being so kind to my son."

And they replied with words similar to what I always hear, "Our pleasure. We were lucky to sit here. Great to meet you, Trevor!"

SERVE FAITHFULLY

Some Christians assume that God chooses prestigious people like Billy Graham or Joni Eareckson Tada when He wants to get important things done, that the rest of us are just filling up space until He returns. Here are three examples from the Bible of formerly insignificant people who achieved lasting significance through their faithful service to God.

Gideon. God called Gideon to rescue Israel from their oppressors, "The Lord is with you, mighty warrior." Gideon doubted his capability, "My clan is the weakest . . . I am the least in my family." And yet Gideon acquired the courage necessary to lead Israel into battle from the time he spent communicating with the Lord. God's vision for Gideon looked beyond his present circumstances and saw the future leader who would lead Israel to a great victory (Judges 6:1–7:25). Trevor also acquires the courage necessary for his job from his daily communication with the Lord.

Nameless servant girl. A Jewish girl was taken captive and became a servant to the wife of Naaman, the commander of the Aramean army who was afflicted with leprosy. This girl could have grown bitter while grumbling against her captors, but instead she embraced the one option always available to anyone whose life seems to be without meaning: faithfully testifying to the healing that can only be found in the God of the Bible. She directed Naaman to the prophet Elisha in Israel, where he received physical and spiritual healing (2 Kings 5:1–16). Trevor could lament about being held "captive" by Down syndrome, but like the servant girl, he uses his predicament to point others to the hope that can only be found through faith in God.

Nameless boy with five loaves and two fishes. The crowd of five thousand men, along with their families, may have disparaged this boy for offering such a meager amount, but at least he had the courage and compassion to give his all in service to God. Jesus took the boy's simple lunch, gave thanks to the Father, had His disciples distribute the food among the crowd, and then everyone ate and was satisfied (Matthew 14:13–21; Mark 6:30–44; John 6:1–13). Jesus can also expand our attempts at service and use them to bless others in our world. The thousands of fans who come through the team stores are spiritually "fed" by Trevor. When they understand who he is, they appreciate what he does and aspire to what he has.

* * *

When the NHL and MLB seasons overlap in the spring and fall, Trevor is concurrently employed by the Angels and the Ducks. He's actually worked a double-header when both teams have had home games scheduled for the same day. So after finishing his first shift at Angel Stadium, he's had to change uniforms in our car while we're driving over to Honda Center for the start of his second shift.

Despite a gravelly voice and sore hands at the end of a ten-hour workday, Trevor still has kind words and high fives for fans straggling in the parking lot as we make our way out to our car. Trevor faithfully follows Jesus' example of kingdom service, which starts when convenience ends and sacrifice begins.

LIVE JOYFULLY

Trevor's joyful personality testifies to corporate officers, famous athletes, sports fans, and other employees of the unquenchable joy that he's found in living for the Lord.

One example of many I could mention occurred during the Angels' 2014 season. As usual, Melissa and I drove up to the stadium, parked our car, and walked over to the employee entrance where we always wait for Trevor to get off work. We've become fairly well acquainted with most of the Angels' security personnel over the years, but the security guard manning the exit on this night was someone whom we'd never met—a large man standing there with his arms folded across his chest.

"How can I help you?" he demanded. "This is not an entrance to the game!"

I replied, "We know. We're waiting for someone."

He insisted, "The players don't come out this way!"

I explained, "We're waiting for our son. He gets off work here fairly soon."

He stated, "Sure. Well, you can't stand here, so please move along!"

I protested, "Please just give us a minute. Wait, I think I hear him coming now!"

The three of us turned and listened to Trevor's energetic cheering echoing from inside the stadium as he made his way out toward the exit. Faintly at first, then growing louder and louder, we could hear him shouting, "Let's go, An-gels! Let's go, An-gels! Let's go, An-gels!"—all while punctuating his cheers with some serious high-fiving of fellow employees that he was passing along the concourse.

The security guard's face had softened to the point of tears by the time he asked us, "So you're Trevor's mom and dad?"

Melissa confirmed, "We are!"

At that very moment, Trevor appeared at the door's entrance, saw the security guard, and exclaimed, "My buddy! Angels are winning!"

Trevor gave a no-doubt long-remembered hug to the security guard, who by then could only croak, "I'm sorry . . . I didn't know . . . I love your son."

I reassured him, "No problem . . . just doing your job. See you tomorrow. God bless."

*   *   *

The first three paragraphs of this postscript explained how the dancing amends I learned to make in my sobriety helped me to be a better dad to Trevor. Conversely, what did I receive from Trevor that has helped me to stay sober for nearly twenty years?

I can answer that question by first answering another one: What does it mean to be Trevorized?

Trevorizing occurs when someone's inspirational influence improves our world and the people living in it. Every place Trevor's feet have walked has been made better by virtue of his presence. Every person Trevor's heart has touched has been made better by virtue of his proximity.

The City of Irvine, Angel Stadium, Honda Center, Voyagers Bible Church, OC Harvest, Vision City Church, Northwood High School, and many other institutions where Trevor's trodden have been blessed through his attendance.

Hundreds of thousands of Angels and Ducks fans, thousands of parishioners, hundreds of classmates, dozens of friends, Melissa, Taylor, and Tanner have all been blessed in proportion to the closeness of the relationship they've enjoyed with Trevor. These places and the people in them have all been Trevorized!

I recall the first time I met Trevor as the happiest, saddest, and greatest day of my life, all in one. Trevor's birth foreshadowed how during our lives together the challenges of synergizing my recovery from alcoholism with the difficulties of his Down syndrome would always draw me closer to God. My life consistently cast shadows during my years of active alcoholism, whereas Trevor's life has continued to consistently shine with the light of God's love. Trevor chooses not to accept the darkness of this world, but instead he drives it out by shining His love everywhere he goes and on everyone he meets. The times I've spent in Trevor's presence are those times when I've felt closest to God. So I guess I've been Trevorized too!

> For you were once darkness, but now you are light in
> the Lord. Live as children of light.
>
> (Ephesians 5:8)

My life no longer casts the shadows it did before I was Trevorized, and yet I'm well aware of how far I still fall short when compared to the "child of light" example Trevor sets with his eternal thinking, faithful serving, and joyful living. I've remained sober for twenty years by striving to assimilate his Trevorizing precepts into my own thoughts, words, and actions:

Thinking eternally is contemplating the knowledge that our sins are forgiven, the promise of our eternal salvation, and the anticipation of spending eternity in heaven with Jesus. Trevor's life demonstrates how God-consciousness eclipses self-consciousness, and therefore he's set free to worship the Lord with all of his heart, soul, mind, and strength.

Serving faithfully is enthusiastically working not only for a paycheck but also to the glory of God. Trevor will never become wealthy from the wages he receives from his jobs, but his life has become a beautiful testimony from what he gives back in his service to the Lord. The world crowns financial success; God crowns faithful service.

Living joyfully will carry us through our brightest days and darkest nights. Some Christians may appear somber and focused on maintaining their dignity—not so with Trevor! The positive cheerfulness he emanates along with the unbridled enthusiasm he radiates come from the joy that overflows from inside his heart.

* * *

Think of the tremendous blessings that would ensue if Christians were always known as happy people with smiles on their faces, encouraging words for everyone, and hugs for the fortunate people in their lives.

Personally pursuing Trevorization should be our first step in that direction, in my humble opinion. Hopefully, Trevorizing will soon be coming to a venue near you, and then you too can be Trevorized by your local greeter with Down syndrome.

If it so unfolds that God's will does not include the national or international expansion of Trevorization but you find yourself in Southern California, then please visit Trevor at Angel Stadium or Honda Center during baseball or hockey season, or stop by Influencers in Irvine on Friday mornings, and you'll be blessed with a front row seat to Trevorizing. Maybe even better yet, as suggested in chapter 8, why not volunteer in your local special-needs community? Imagine the spiritual blessings that would develop not only in the lives of the special-needs individuals wherever you live but also in regard to the Trevorizing of your own heart, soul, mind, and body.

After you've been duly Trevorized, then it follows that you in turn will be free to Trevorize your own world. Your home, school, workplace, neighborhood, and every place you wander in life will be spiritually improved from your presence. Your spouse, children, family, friends, classmates, coworkers, and even strangers on the street whose hearts your life has touched will be blessed through your interaction in their lives.

Think eternally, serve faithfully, and live joyfully.

—Trevor William Hendershot

Trevorizing Influencers Men's Group in Irvine, California

NOTES

1. Marcia Smith, "Angels Give Down Syndrome Man a Chance," *Orange County Register,* Apr. 17, 2012, http://www.ocregister.com/article/angels-349578-hendershot-trevor.html.

2. Marcia Smith, "Greeter Provides Service with a Smile," *Orange County Register,* Apr. 15, 2013, http://www.ocregister.com/articles/angels-504236-hendershot-ducks.html.

3. Emily Perl Kingsley, "Welcome to Holland" (1987), http://www.our-kids.org/Archives/Holland.html.

4. Influencers, http://www.influencerswest.org.

5. Celebrate Recovery, http://www.celebraterecovery.com.

6. *Alcoholics Anonymous, Third Edition* (NY: Alcoholics Anonymous World Services, 1976), 216–217.

7. *Alcoholics Anonymous, Fourth Edition* (NY: Alcoholics Anonymous World Services, 2001), 83–84.

8. Anschutz Entertainment Group, http://www.aegworldwide.com.

ADDITIONAL RESOURCES

http://www.angelsforhigher.org

http://www.ocregister.com/articles/trevor-695682-hendershot-team.html. Marcia Smith, "Special-needs Son Turns Father's Anger into Unabashed Pride – Maybe Even Saving His Life in the Process," *Orange County Register,* Dec. 11, 2015.

Stay connected with Robert and Trevor:

- Facebook – Robert Hendershot and Trevor Hendershot
- Twitter – @AngelsforHigher
- Instagram – @rmhendershot
- LinkedIn – Robert Hendershot (Writer)

Made in the USA
Lexington, KY
23 April 2017